Bubble UP Church

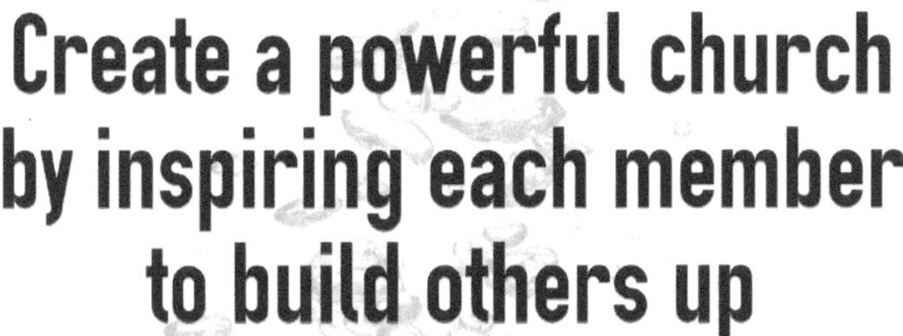

Create a powerful church by inspiring each member to build others up

Gary and Wendy Carter

Published by: Kainos Enterprises
7777 Churchville Road
Brampton ON L6Y 0H3

ISBN-13: 978-0-9685427-5-0

Free Bonus!

Bubble UP Church Resources

At least $30 value for you free!

Email: resources@kainos.org

for instant access links.

Contents

Stop It!

Finish It!

Foreword

"I do not envision that this blast of my trumpet will bring down the walls of pseudo-science which are manned by too many stout defenders. Nevertheless, there are still some people about who like to use their brains... and it is for them that this book is intended."

I came across this statement by Stanislav Andreski the other day. I thought to myself, that this best describes this book by Gary & Wendy Carter. They are writing from two lifetimes of experience in churches across Canada and the stories they tell are illustrative of that. I am sure they would love to know that some walls of indifference, complacency and plain old Christian lethargy will tumble once this book is released into the pews and backyards of the nation. May it be so!

I would caution any reader of this book to read it slowly. Don't make the mistake of sitting down and reading it at one time. It is meant, at least in my mind, to be read slowly. Give yourself time to digest the truths as they are distilled before you. Even doing it in a small group would be a better way to read it. While there are over 200 scripture references the value is seen in the way the truths are applied and the questions that are asked of us, the Reader. Skimming the book will be counterproductive.

I am reminded of a quote from Will Rogers, who once said "If stupidity got us in this mess, then why can't it get us out?" I feel that expresses what is happening in so many churches across North America these days. We are simply making some stupid decisions and we are paying a high price for Kingdom advancement. If the Church is the only means by which the Lord envisioned to impact this world – and it is – why are we making such little impact? If you wish to succeed in your church your journey must begin by asking the right questions. They are often hard to ask, especially among friends and people you have known for years. But you will never arrive at the right solutions without asking them. This book will challenge you to do that.

I especially enjoyed the chapter on Forgiveness. Forgiveness is not re-framing the offense to a lesser category. Dealing with three kinds of offenses – inadvertent, indirect and intentional, gives one pause for contemplation. That is why one must read this book slowly to reap the benefit.

Of all the books the Carters have written, this is their best. Let it impact your soul!

Dr. Warwick Cooper

Dr. Warwick Cooper has an undergraduate degree in Theology from Northwest Baptist College in Vancouver, BC, an MA from Providence Seminary in Manitoba and a DMin from Andersonville Baptist Seminary in Atlanta. He has been a Pastor and a Marriage and Family Counselor since 1985.

Dr. Cooper has pastored 5 churches in Canada and has worked as the Pastor of Counseling and Family Ministries at The Peoples Church in Toronto since 2001. He manages 5 other Counselors and 11 ministries working in the community in the area of divorce recovery, family counselling, parenting classes, grief, addictions and sexual identity issues. He is a member of the Ontario Association of Consultants, Counselors, & Psychomtertrists (OACCP), The American Association of Biblical Counselors (AABC),and the American Association of Christian Counselors (AACC).

Introduction

Timmy exclaimed, "I'm really hungry, Mommy!" as his round bulging three-year-old eyes peered over the edge of the kitchen table. Those eyes were looking straight at the mound of scrumptious-smelling pancakes sitting near a bottle of yummy maple syrup. His mom responded, "Well, just get your body up on the bench and you can share in some breakfast with me." "OK Mommy!" Timmy readily agreed.

It's time the people in your church had such a craving for living out God's inspired Word. Many are missing out on all the wonderful topics of behavior change to study in the Bible. One of these is the particular subject we have chosen for this book on all the "*one anothers*" in the Bible.

This is a first! Gary and Wendy have both written books before. But this is our first one together. We have worked on over a score of books. But generally in our other books one of us did the writing and the other did the critiquing and editing. This is different because you will hear each of our voices. Until now the books we have written are under one name or the other and others are "ghost written" for other people.

But it's time.

Let's explain about ourselves. Wendy is the practical one. Gary would have his head in the clouds if it weren't for Wendy. But then Wendy would stick to mundane routines if Gary didn't encourage her to explore new ideas. Now that is not absolute. Wendy has vision. And Gary can proofread too.

Wendy has added the human color to the book. Her stories from life situations are like starter fluid into many of the chapters. You will notice that most of her stories have something to do with life in the church and then some in our family. These stories will point your mind in a good direction.

Gary adds more of the philosophical stuff. He attempts to get you to think about how life could be in your church. For both of us it is all about church because *"Christ loved the church and gave himself up for her."* (Ephesians 5:25)

The healthy church must be a synergistic interaction of people. It is all about the people. Church programs, systems, structures and buildings are all important, but more attention must be given to the people. Leadership is critical. The leaders must follow Christ and model behavior from the top down. We can think of that as, "Trickle Down Church." There are lots of books on that. But there are all too few that put the spotlight on how the church must grow from the bottom up. Ordinary people can change any church if enough of them live right. That is what we call, "Bubble UP Church." It is too easy for the leaders to lambaste the followers and the followers to criticize the leaders. Each can make the other more successful if the Christian life is lived out properly. That is our premise. And we will take this journey together.

In the following pages, once we get past the "Dig It!" and the next "Wrote It!" sections you will notice the format in each chapter has a "Wendy's Take" section followed by a "Gary's Take" section. Then the final section is "Your Take." That is where the fun begins because we ask you to think practically and personally about your role in church.

Dig It!

Bubble UP Church is set out in several sections to keep the general thought flowing. The main chapters are each based on the relevant uses of the Greek term for "*one another*" found throughout the New Testament. The first two sections set the stage for us and the last section ties it all together. The middle sections make reasonable clusters of the "*one another*" concepts.

~1~
Church Vitality

Famously, a writer of long ago (Henry David Thoreau) wrote, "The mass of men lead lives of quiet desperation. What is called resignation is confirmed desperation." That is a heavy statement Thoreau wrote in 1846. If it was true then it must be at least equally true today.

In quiet polite conversation many observe that the church of today is in a state of resignation or confirmed desperation. The exception seems to be the cool big churches with all the splash. The way to go today that catches the buzz is the multi-site church with the famous front man or woman. The rest of us languish beside Walden Pond with Thoreau.

Nonsense. It is not all that bad in the non-mega church. In fact, it is not all that good in the mega-church. Go ahead look for that big church in the Bible. You won't find the necessity of all the equipment right down to the countdown timer on the back wall. It used to be a clock; now it is a large screen with all the cues. You won't find the timer in the Bible either. But you will find everything you need there. *"His divine power has given us everything we need for a godly life through our knowledge of him who called us by his own glory and goodness."* (2 Peter 1:3) Maybe Thoreau had it correct; Peter had it inspired!

There is no need for quiet desperation in your church. There is a need for divine power, not media savvy. Divine power is provided in abundance for right living. Right living is the issue. Right living is what we are called to. Don't aspire to be bigger; aspire to be better and growth will follow. New stuff won't give you the boost you need in your church anywhere near as effectively as a divine power boost in the people. Bubble up the character first. However, the organization will change in due time because of the changes in the individuals.

Let's cover something important for the reader who has a foggy idea about what we mean by church. A church is a local gathering of people with distinct characteristics. First and foremost the people gather at different times and perhaps in different places. The location is a convenience, not an essential. The gathering is essential. These gatherings have three components. The gathered people have a sense of belonging; they have shared beliefs and they have common behavior patterns with moral direction.

The churches to which we speak have four common belief patterns. They believe the Bible is foundational and the only ultimate authority on the subjects to which it speaks. They believe the historic events of Jesus' death, burial and resurrection are the centerpiece of history. They have profound impact on all societies whether or not those peoples agree. They believe there must be a personal transaction between every human and God. In this transaction the individual places complete trust in this afore mentioned work of Christ. This belief creates Jesus as their personal life leader in all action and morality. They believe that the church ought to exist primarily for those who aren't a part of it yet. Thus the church must be active in the world in evangelism, missionary work and social responsibility. This means churches are not merely clubs for the current insiders. They accept that they must reach and impact others who may or may not believe or come to believe as they do.

Often the concept communicated is of a group of people meeting in one place at one time. Several references speak of this as a daily, weekly or a regularly repeated occurrence. When people get together for any cause it binds them to each other. This is never more true than in the church. The New Testament never contemplates the possibility of a believer who doesn't meet with the group of like-minded people in their local area. There are no hermit Christians in the Book. While media of all kinds help us in many ways there is no substitution for human face-to-face events. No invention from the printing press to the telephone has changed this fact. Nothing invented since then and into the future will change the need for people to be with people in church.

Those were three weighty paragraphs. If it is unclear to you then we are not on the same page yet as to what the church is all about. For you – if you find this unclear – the rest of what is to follow will have a measure of detachment for you. At the same time, we hope you will find it compelling. The church is a wonderful place of rescue for broken people designed by God as a healing, life-giving place with authentic relationships and support.

In our experience in churches, large and small, we have noticed an important phenomenon. The church seldom follows the lead pastor anywhere near as much as it follows the people who follow the pastor's lead. Did you catch that? It is the few key participants who gather around the pastor and follow that make all the difference. The church follows the second man, not the first. The lead pastor may be the most enthusiastic and articulate. He may have great vision. He may have a solid action plan. But if he doesn't have one, two or three trusted influencers who point to him and in effect say, "What he said!" the church will not thrive.

When a church doesn't have a good example in the lead pastor then those key influencers cannot in good conscience aspire to be like him. They will need to lay back and pray that others who grasp the pastor's soul, style and methods will step into the gap.

However, even in a place where the leadership core is suspect, every individual can make a significant positive impact if they choose to. This is a book about that. It is a book for every believer.

Even though this book is for every believer, there is a great deal to say about leadership. After all, every pastor and key influencer ought to be able to say with Paul, *"Follow my example, as I follow the example of Christ."* (1 Corinthians 11:1) Jesus himself gave specific instructions about how to follow him. They are worth your study. Anyone who doesn't strive to live these out ought not to be in church leadership.

Open your Bible and read the story around the key verse listed.

1. Follow & Fish.. Matthew 4:19
   "Come, follow me," Jesus said, "and I will send you out to fish for people."
   Do I bring people to Jesus?

2. Follow & Focus.. Matthew 8:22
   "But Jesus told him, 'Follow me, and let the dead bury their own dead.'"
   Do I set family and business concerns behind following Jesus?

3. Follow & Facilitate.. Matthew 9:9
   "As Jesus went on from there, he saw a man named Matthew sitting at the tax collector's booth. 'Follow me,' he told him, and Matthew got up and followed him."
   Do I bring people to meetings where they can meet Jesus?

4. Follow & Forfeit.. Matthew 10:38
   "Whoever does not take up their cross and follow me is not worthy of me."
   .... Matthew 16:24
   "Then Jesus said to his disciples, 'Whoever wants to be my disciple must deny themselves and take up their cross and follow me.'"
   Do I set my personal agenda aside so I can follow Jesus closer?

5. Follow & Finance.. Matthew 19:21
   "Jesus answered, 'If you want to be perfect, go, sell your possessions and give to the poor, and you will have treasure in heaven. Then come, follow me.'"
   Do I put following Jesus before money?

6. Follow & Find ....John 1:43
   "The next day Jesus decided to leave for Galilee. Finding Philip, he said to him, 'Follow me.'"
   Do I seek to find people to follow Jesus with me?

7. Follow & Fellowship..John 10:27
   "My sheep listen to my voice; I know them, and they follow me."
   Do I listen to Jesus through his Word every day?

8. Follow & Farm ....John 12:26
   "Whoever serves me must follow me; and where I am, my servant also will be. My Father will honor the one who serves me."
   Do I let the seeds I plant die so they can multiply for Jesus?

9. Follow & Finish...John 21:19
   "Jesus said this to indicate the kind of death by which Peter would glorify God. Then he said to him, 'Follow me!'"
   Will I finish strong in following Jesus?

10. Follow & Fixate..John 21:22

"Jesus answered, 'If I want him to remain alive until I return, what is that to you? You must follow me.'"
Do I mind my own business as I follow Jesus?

If you are a leader, check up on yourself and make sure you get with the program. If you are not a leader, you get with the program and set an example and perhaps the leaders will join you in following Jesus as they should. Bubble the example up from the bottom!

Now, let's be clear, scolding people seldom brings people to their senses. Providing living proof does.

The New Testament has over 400 verses that give explicit direct instruction on how to get your act together. You won't get your act together by concentrating on better music and preaching. There we said it. Had you wondered about that? There is some – but not much – instruction about music and preaching. There is a trainload of practical instruction on how to shape your personality by grace and obedience. The good news is that divine power is already available for the personality tweaks we all need through Christ.

Of those 400 Bible verses approximately one out of ten talks about our direct relationship with the Lord and how we focus our attention on him. About four out of those ten verses concentrate on our personal inner life and outer behavior. You won't pay attention to that if you are singing your favorite ValleySong piece over and over. You will if you know how to get yourself to pay attention. We are about to cover some of that. But the largest category of Bible commands in the New Testament concentrate our attention on how we treat each other.

There is one word in the Koiné Greek language in which the New Testament is written that is used many times to refer to how we treat each other. It is usually translated with two English words "*one another*." That word is the anchor to all the chapters that follow. It speaks of our reciprocal responsibility to each other in the church. It doesn't speak of a hierarchy of people. There are some biblical indications that we all have a responsibility to respond to appropriate leadership but this word points us in another direction as well. Leadership counts. There are many places to go to find information about leadership. There aren't as many places we can find to put the spotlight on reciprocal relationships. Start with the Greek word "*allélón*" pronounced "al-lay-lone."

People in churches become disengaged because of a failure in relationships far more often than they do because of a failure of programming, performance, building, organizational structure, music or preaching.

All churches leak. People leave because they move away, fall off and die off. By the time they are out the door it is often too late to notice. Those who fall off do so before it becomes obvious in their attendance patterns. In many churches nobody notices the fall off. And in many of those, even when they notice they don't do anything about it before it is too late. Quiet desperation rears its ugly head.

When the church leads with attention to reciprocal relationships the church starts to bubble up. Fewer people walk away. More people invite others to church. People find the Lord because they find friends at church first. It is easier for one to accept someone calling them a "sinner" when they know that person knows and cares about them. If a person doesn't get to understand their lost estate they won't find salvation.

We cannot allow the world to think of us as the people who are all about prohibiting bad behavior. We are about promoting a lifestyle that is attractive and compelling. We are about activating churches in communities, not about fighting others or other churches. Once you think through all this material you will agree that outsiders should be beating down our doors to belong to such a positive group of people who supply hope and comfort for time and eternity.

~ 2 ~

Church and Personal Self-Esteem

If someone were to say to you, "Tell me about your church." how would you respond?

Your brain might scramble in many directions before your mouth starts to speak. Where would you start? You could tell about the building, the pastor, the meetings or the people you know at church. If you started with the meetings, you probably would start with the main meeting. That usually occurs on Sunday morning but you might start with a meeting at some other time of the week.

You are likely to start with your opinion of something about your church or at least reveal your attitude in the way you talk. If your church is big you will reveal your evaluation in how you say, "big." If you like "big" you will say it with pride. If "big" is "too big" for you and you feel detached you will say it with some regret or tentativeness. If your church is "small" and you think "small" is not good, you will broadcast it in your tone. But then who says your church is small? How small is small after all?

Whatever you say about your church you will say it to get an intended effect. You might pretend a bit to encourage someone to like your church. You probably will, as the saying goes, put your best foot forward. It is complicated to tell the truth about a church without telling the nastier side of the truth. On the other hand, your church has many laudable characteristics you probably won't mention because you take them for granted.

Frankly, some churches overestimate themselves because the participants dwell on the wrong things. Church leaders are too concerned about performance, organizational structure and even physical structural elements. The Bible has little to say about organization and nothing to tell you how to build a building.

The Bible has a lot to say about becoming better people. The content of the character is much more important than the container. The insides sneak out the cracks over time. When leaders show the right character, attitude and approach it bubbles out to others. When others see the effervescent bubbling of the right characteristics, they love it and then find inspiration to live out a bubbling life as well.

All churches could get better. And we have never visited a church that was as bad as it could be.

Starting with you, the reader, we will confidently assert that your church will get better when you get a little better. And when you get a little better, others are likely to follow your example. That will make your church a whole lot better no matter what! However, if you only read this for knowledge or cognitive information nothing will change. Each of us must have attitude change which leads to behavioral evolution or even revolution. To do that we all have to lasso our wills, associate with other believers who help us forward and restructure the way we approach life. And such development will only happen as we let the Lord write it on our hearts by grace. If we don't we will just say we are too busy or use some other lame excuse.

On the pages that follow we are going to set aside everything else and focus on you. You cannot change another human; you can only work on yourself. With the work of grace, there is no telling how far you can go with the time you have left on earth. That is because your example will live on long after your life in your church has ended. Your connection to your church might end because you move on out or it might end because you move on up to Glory.

~ 3 ~
The Inspired Authors

The key word we are going to track through the New Testament is "*al-lélón*" which is usually translated "*one another*" or "*each other.*" There are 100 occurrences of this word but not all of them apply to the Christian life. These incidental uses are set aside. But there are 62 uses we are going to look at. Several are repeated so when we eliminate the duplicates there are 36 different concepts to adhere to. There are a variety of ways in the New Testament to refer to the relationships among people but we have a specific focus on one word.

It is impossible to live out what we are going to talk about outside of a group context. This is true because each concept requires one person relating to others in the same way.

Now, don't panic! We don't have long chapters and a few are grouped together so we can give a cursory examination of them all.

This one word "*one another*" doesn't collect all the Bible has to say about how we must relate to each other but it gives us a great start.

Jesus most famously used "*one another*" with the word "*love*" three times in two verses. He declares that he is giving a new command. Listen. "*A new command I give you: Love one another. As I have loved you, so you must love one another. By this everyone will know that you are my disciples, if you love one another.*" (John 13:34-35) I find most people can read that but not understand that his new command is not about loving people outside the family of God so that they are compelled to join. No. He is saying they will only know that we are the real deal when they see brothers and sisters loving each other. That requires getting unbelievers into a context where they can observe Christian love among believers in action. He is not telling us here to witness on the streets; he is telling us to allow unbelievers to watch for our love in the house.

Peter used the word four times. He repeated Jesus' message about "*love one another*" once showing he got the message. Some might argue that it took Peter some time to give his loving attention to others in his thought processes and his behaviors. Incidents in the Gospels give us clues that Peter was self-centered. Mark a close associate of Peter used the word once,

John used the word 14 times. Six of these times he said "*love one another.*" He really got the message! Maybe watching Peter learn the lesson slowly put it in his frontal lobes. Just speculating.

Now Paul, he was the "*one another*" king. He used the word 37 times. He used it once every 875 words; whereas John used it once every 4013 words. Paul didn't repeat himself very often. He had many things to say about how we must conduct ourselves with "*one another.*"

Had you thought of James yet? He used the target word four times and that was once every 435 words. Probably James was the brother of Jesus who came to faith after the resurrection. He doesn't quote the "*one another*" word with the word "*love*" like Jesus and John did, but he did understand that we need to relate to each other in the church.

The only author left is the writer of Hebrews. We don't know who that was. And he only used the term twice.

This is an important study about obeying everything Jesus commanded as the Great Commission requires. Of course, the frequency of the use of the word isn't the whole story. But the fact that the word emphasizes our relationships with fellow believers is most significant. We need to pay attention!

~ 4 ~
One Anothering

This word *"one another"* is simple enough in itself. But if we don't think long and hard about it, we might let it slip on by without giving it enough attention. So let's break it down starting with the obvious.

This is about human relationships. It all starts with one. One person is all that matters. Well, that is one at a time. It is too easy to hide in the crowd. If in a crowd the leader says, "Everyone with the name John please raise your hand." only some hands go up. Tom, Dick and Harry don't raise their hands because their name is not John. The leader is making the request of a subset of the whole group. Of course, nobody in the room is named "One." But if the leader asked, "Everyone who is human raise your hand." people would give back a quizzical look, not a raised hand. Everyone is human. But perhaps everyone in the room isn't a true believer. So if the leader asks, "Everyone in the room who is a blood-bought saint who knows their sins are forgiven and who can say without a doubt they are a fully devoted follower of Jesus please stand up." a few may not stand up. It is those who are standing that this word is about. Every Christian must take this word seriously or they don't truly qualify as a Christian.

The word *"one another"* is about the human relationships among fellow Christians. It isn't about a general sense of love for all humanity. Therefore, every believer is under the obligation to relate to other Christians. Sadly, about half of the people who might tell you they are a Christian only randomly come in contact with others who also say they are Christians. In fact, many of that half deliberately avoid others who say they are Christians. It is impossible to live out any one of these "*one anothers*" without intentional activity to get to the same place at the same time as other Christians. Further, the getting together must involve contact. Eye contact. Speaking contact. Physical contact. Real contact.

This is a real issue about following Jesus. The Bible never contemplates the possibility of an unattached Christian as a viable option. When someone tells you they are a follower of Jesus but they have given up on church they must be confused. Perhaps they thought the church was going to be a place where everything works out perfectly because everyone agrees with each other. That is not only an unrealistic expectation; it is totally contrary to how the Bible describes the church for which Jesus died. The church had its problems right out of the box.

There was a magnificent start as recorded in Acts 2. But by Acts 5 they started to have problems. Anyone who seriously reads the Bible for instruction about what to expect in church will realize that much of the New Testament is written to correct problems in the church. And the problems were overwhelmingly relational. Relationships always need some work. You can't follow Jesus and not have some days when things aren't totally comfortable between you and others. Running away will never solve your problems. You take them with you wherever you go in this world. The next world is the place which is pain free. There is no medication that will eliminate the pain of living side by side with other Christians. The good news is that we have solid instructions on how to get things fixed. The thing is, it is all about getting ourselves fixed. We can never fix another human being. They can only fix themselves by grace.

The bulk of this book draws attention to exactly how believers must behave with each other. The words and phrases are very specific. Each one brings a different facet to the relationships. These phrases give every soul a good working over! They beat us all up because we aren't as good at it as we could be. But before we take ourselves to the cleaners there is more to say.

We all have a bit of the "Dunning–Kruger Effect" operating in us. These two psychologists proposed that people who are ignorant or unskilled in a given domain tend to believe they are much more competent than they are. Tone deaf people sing along blissfully because they can't tell they are tone deaf. Bad drivers don't agree they lack driving skill. Our own incompetencies lead us all to tend to start with overstated self-assessment. Underdeveloped Christians think they are more developed than they are. Interestingly, under-developed Christians consider themselves as good judges of others way too often. They themselves would be willing to behave better if others did so first with them. They would be more loving if others were more loving. Seldom is their assessment accurate.

On the "*one another*" street it seems as if there are several lanes of traffic on our side of the road each representing different behaviors. We give out to others driving in our lanes. But it seems there is only one skinny lane coming in the other direction representing what others do for us. If we see it as two arrows going in opposite directions our arrow looks big to us and the other person's arrow looks much smaller. In a household, ask the children which one of them contributes most to the family chores and they may all raise their hands. They know what they do but don't see what the other family members contribute to the good of the whole. In ill-formed and undisciplined families the adults take care of the children completely. Then the children expect such entitlement to be their due because they are special.

We could extend that understanding to the whole society around us. Workers are always worth more than they are paid and owners all pay too much tax to the government. Those workers would work harder if they were paid more. Those owners would be happy to pay their taxes if the government didn't waste so much money. Wanna bet? The world around us is full of takers with all too few givers. The takers often will tell you they will meet you halfway and become matchers. This is off topic but don't ever believe a taker will become a matcher because they tell you they are willing to meet you in the middle. You will likely have a different definition of where the middle ground is.

Life will continue to get you down if you think that some day in some way you will have it your own way. This "*one another*" business is all about me being the best me in my traffic lane. Christians and those who say they are Christians are bound to disappoint you. There will come times when you wonder if the person on the other side of the relationship that is troubling you even knows the Lord at all. Maybe they don't, Jesus said the crowd of people on the outside who thought they were on the inside will be great. *"Not everyone who says to me, 'Lord, Lord,' will enter the kingdom of heaven, but only the one who does the will of my Father who is in heaven. Many will say to me on that day, 'Lord, Lord, did we not prophesy in your name and in your name drive out demons and in your name perform many miracles?' Then*

I will tell them plainly, 'I never knew you. Away from me, you evildoers!" (Matthew 7:21-23)

Your church doesn't need any participants overcome by the Dunning-Kruger Effect. Wait. Actually it does. Those people need you to set a different example so they can see what it is to grow in Christ. You might wish everyone would give more than they do. You have a point. But you can't control how much "*one anothering*" others do. You can control your own activity. So if you are ready to come to the cleaners with us, let's get to it.

~ 5 ~

Love One Another

"A new command I give you: Love one another. As I have loved you, so you must love one another. By this everyone will know that you are my disciples, if you love one another."* *(John 13:34-35, also John 15:12, John 15:17, Romans 13:8, 1 Thessalonians 3:12, 1 Thessalonians 4:9, 2 Thessalonians 1:3, 1 Peter 1:22, 1 John 3:11, 1 John 3:23, 1 John 4:7, 1 John 4:11, 1 John 4:12, 2 John 1:5)

The phrase "*love one another*" is the granddaddy of them all. The exact phrase "*love one another*" is used 14 times in the New Testament. The word "*love*" is used in 21 verses where the other word "*one another*" shows up. And in these verses the word "*love*" is used 32 times.

Actually, there are 62 relevant uses of the term "*one another*" that flesh out what this love means. This book is built on them. There are some places in the New Testament where the concept of each other is expounded using other words. We don't cover any of those. There is quite enough to think about here for now without attempting to be exhaustive.

Do you think the Bible is trying to tell us something? It should be noted that only two of these verses include how we relate to "all people" or to our "neighbor." There is plenty to say about loving our neighbors in the Bible but not in the verses where the words "*love*" and "*one another*" are combined. Between 15 and 20% of New Testament commands speak to how believers relate to non-believers. So that too is an important subject. But it isn't much of a "*one another*" subject.

The world is saturated with content that attempts to talk about love. They miss the point 99.9% of the time. But there is something to it. The feelings people associate with love are generated by chemicals in response to life events. We are not experts on hormones and neurotransmitters so we won't dig in very far on specifics. You can do your own research; knowledge is expanding every day.

Some chemicals are thought to be created exclusively or predominantly in the brain. Others are created in other parts of our bodies. (For example, "testosterone" and "estrogen" are produced in the male gonads and the female ovaries. Males produce "estrogen" through a chemical process converting "testosterone." There are several hormones and neurotransmitters produced in the brain. You can research "epinephrine" or "adrenaline", "norepinephrine" or "noradrenaline", "endorphins", "dopamine", "serotonin", and "oxytocin." Each has a part to play in how we think, feel and behave. And there are dozens of other such chemicals. Various drugs (both legal and illicit) are used to replace or mimic the natural function of these chemicals. That is because humans face the need to improve their living by thinking, feeling and behaving better. Several of these chemicals have a role to play in how we experience feelings associated with happiness, wholeness, fondness, joy, pride, status, fulfillment, friendship, attraction, sexuality and so on. Everyone wants a better life and more of all these. When life is in chemical balance we don't get hooked on anything or depressed about too many things. When life is in chemical imbalance we all get out of kilter. As we age we produce smaller amounts of these chemicals to motivate us and so we have to learn to push ourselves with our will much more. Learn the art of controlling your will early in life and it will stand you in good stead when things start to wane after about age 50.

What's love got to do with all that?

Love is not fundamentally a feeling. The feelings are chemical responses to situations, events and relationships. Loving activities produce the feelings. The feelings don't produce love. But after all, the Christian life is experience and we should pay attention to the legitimate release of feel-good chemistry. We should pay attention to all the senses in the church. Sight and sound are the senses du jour. And they don't just happen on a platform. We need to attend to smell, taste and touch as well. That is a whole other subject to explore for another day.

The Greek words for love are "eros" or sexual engagement, "*phileo*" or friendship "storge" or family-type affection and "*agape*." The four words were popularized by the classic book "The Four Loves" by C.S. Lewis published in 1960. The words "eros" and "storge" aren't in the Bible. But there are a few compound words containing "storge." For example, "*a-storge*" which means simply unloving. "*Philia*" is used 25 times with a variety of meanings. But its compound use in "*philadelphia*" is used six times. That is a great word combining "*philia*" or friendship and "*adelphos*" or brother. Philadelphia is supposed to be about friendships in the church or among the brothers and sisters.

The biggee word is "*agape*." It is used 116 times in the New Testament in the noun form and 143 times in the verb form. There are dozens of other words with the same root. This is the self-sacrificing love that is unconditional. By this love the lover donates self, time and effort on behalf of creating the true well-being of others regardless of their worth to receive such attention. All the other loves pale in comparison to this love. All of the other loves are held subservient to this "*agape*." That is the deal.

When a believer chooses the self-donation of time, effort and money for the great cause of the Kingdom of God through the relationships of the people of God, that is love. The emotional side we think of as love will surely follow the self-sacrifice. Love makes you feel good but feeling good in itself is not love.

John said it best, *"Dear friends, let us love one another, for love comes from God. Everyone who loves has been born of God and knows God. Whoever does not love does not know God, because God is love. This is how God showed his love among us: He sent his one and only Son into the world that we might live through him. This is love: not that we loved God, but that he loved us and sent his Son as an atoning sacrifice for our sins. Dear friends, since God so loved us, we also ought to love one another. No one has ever seen God; but if we love one another, God lives in us and his love is made complete in us."* (1 John 4:7-12)

Drop the mic.

Start It!

The chapters in this section are where it all begins as we start to flesh out the concept "*love one another.*" These concepts are selected because if we can't get these right it will be impossible to build the church we long for. Each of us has to change for the church to experience real Godly change. The cumulative effect of small changes is astounding but we all have to begin and continue to do the right things.

~ 6 ~

Hello World

"Greet one another with a kiss of love. Peace to all of you who are in Christ."* *(1 Peter 5:14, also Romans 16:16, 1 Corinthians 16:20, 2 Corinthians 13:12)

It all starts at "Hello." And continued conversations won't follow if you don't start somewhere. Trace every important relationship you have ever had in life back to its very beginning. Notice you can usually come very close to the actual first conversation or maybe even remember it exactly. What started it? One of you said the first word. Probably the first words you ever heard were uttered by your mother. After a while you learned to respond to your mother with goos and giggles. That was your first, "Hello" moment. More of those leads you to more new relationships.

Wendy's Take

Greeting cards for birthdays, anniversaries, Christmas, sickness or sympathy are not used as often today as they once were. That's too bad because everyone loves to receive mail. Somehow the e-card just doesn't cut it. I remember being excited about getting a post card from my Sunday School teacher as a child when I was away for whatever reason. In a large church we attended one elderly widower sends out a lot of cards throughout the year to the friends he has made. It shows he cares by his extra thought and effort. Two ladies from the seniors ministry are constantly being thanked by those who have received one of their cards. It is an added bonus that goes beyond the repetitive "hello" Sunday mornings.

I am associated with a card company that provides thousands of card choices online. I choose a card for a special occasion, add a photo if I wish, create a message with my signature and all this information is sent to their processing plant. My information is printed on a real physical card. They address the envelope, put a real stamp on it, and send it on its way to my friend or family member. And I don't have to spend extra time at a store looking for a special card. It has become my signature piece through the years for which many have thanked me. They know that I have been thinking of them and am concerned about what is happening in their lives. In return they can keep track of what Gary and I are up to these days with my quick note.

Gary's Take

Four times in the New Testament there is the command to *"greet one another with a kiss."* Three times it is a "*holy kiss*" and once it is "*a kiss of love*." This command "*greet one another*" is given by Paul to two different churches and to a third church Paul encourages, *"Greet all God's people with a holy kiss."* Interestingly, in all five cases this command comes at the end of five different letters. Don't pay too much attention to the word "*kiss*" just yet. The key word is "*greet*."

The last chapter of Romans is unique among Paul's writings. In it he uses the term *"greet"* 22 times. In most cases where he mentions an individual he draws attention to a characteristic of the individual. It is obvious he knew these people in the church at Rome. There are back stories we don't know. My favorite is, "*Greet Rufus, chosen in the Lord, and his mother, who has been a mother to me, too.*" (Romans 16:13) Why was Rufus singled out as one "*chosen in the Lord"*? They were all chosen. There must have been something remarkable about Rufus' salvation story. And then there is his mom. What is up with that? When did she mother Paul? This was so personal, as it must have been in every case.

Paul and Peter both make mention of sharing greetings from the network where they were currently engaged. They mention names and churches. On a couple of occasions we know the churches happened to meet in the houses of individuals mentioned. Even at a distance, greetings among brothers and sisters were shared.

The word "*warm*" is often used with the word *"greet"* in the context of these instructions on greeting at the end of the letters. The instruction to greet is usually in the context of a few final pithy instructions about peace, holding to what is good, devotion, encouragement and unity. It feels like a hovering mother leaving her children at someone's house and giving them final instructions about how to behave. She wants the very best out of her kids. You can feel Paul and Peter yearning for these people in the churches to do one better than just getting along. These apostles urgently long for the people of God to care for each other in the strongest of ways.

In this context the word "*kiss*" makes total sense. It was the culturally appropriate way to greet for them. It was holy. There was something specially set apart about this greeting. It isn't simply an avoidance of sexual stimulation although it includes that. Our brain chemistry has a fine line between friendship attraction and sexual attraction; therefore we must always be careful not to get the wrong motor started. In this *"one another"* business there has to be warm connection among believers. Hugs and kisses as appropriate but most certainly use eye contact, facial expression and vocal tone with emotion and enthusiasm.

Not many *"one anothers"* are repeated in the New Testament. "*Greet one another*" is a notable exception. How we start the day with each other is really important. And you can't do that properly if you don't get in the house before the meeting starts. The standard greeter at the door is supposed to be nice about it. Good. However, every believer is supposed to be there warmly greeting people all the time when they don't have a special assignment. Better. Much better. There are no instructions about setting up the room for the meeting. The best set up for any meeting is the greeting of people. The best time to greet people is as they arrive.

Every time there is a church meeting every believer needs to be fully engaged for the meeting to succeed. Everyone has to lean in to the experience of being together in the same place at the same time. This is a time to meet your friends and it is a time to meet friends you haven't met yet.

In rather extensive research we have conducted with people who don't yet attend church, the number one thing they say they would be looking for if they were to attend is friends. They want to connect. They often have delicate needs. On the one hand, they want connection and on the other they are hesitant to connect. They aren't sure if they will be welcomed as equals. And nobody likes to be rejected.

Make it your aim to look for people you haven't met yet every time you attend a meeting. Take initiative to say hello to these people in addition to your friends. After all, a stranger is merely a friend you haven't met yet.

Your Take

1. What is your Sunday routine to make sure you arrive long before the meeting begins so you can greet?
2. What do you do to get the others in your household in the right mood to create greeting warmth in your church?
3. How do you get yourself to go out of your way to greet people you don't know well?

~7~

Let's Talk

"Offer hospitality to one another without grumbling." (1 Peter 4:9)

Front porches are made for visiting. On a summer evening neighbors drop by to chat. A world without porches is a world of isolation. The church should be a front porch kind of place. A glass of juice and a cookie might be nice. But it is the conversation that is remembered for a long time. Pull up a chair and let's chat about that.

Wendy's Take

Hospitality isn't really my thing. I am not a cook; although through the years I have convinced my children and now most of our eleven grandchildren that I can bake an unforgettable apple pie. As with anything else the more you do it, the more comfortable you become. Early on in our marriage I remember asking friends over for cinnamon toast after an evening church service. Even though very simple, the warm relationship that developed was far worth the endeavor. The concept of hospitality must be important for it is mentioned several times in the New Testament.

One of the easiest ways to show hospitality is to invite a friend out for a coffee or if you are feeling more magnanimous meet a couple at a restaurant for lunch. However inviting someone over to your home counts for more.

Many people ask me why I am so quiet. I guess I am a contrast to my husband, Gary, who likes to passionately expound on the things he cares about. Actually a lot have learned much from him. I do prefer listening but if I have something to say I will say it. If we invite people into our home then they can get the real picture of who we are as a family. Our heritage home was built in 1837 near the Credit River in the village of Churchville in Brampton, Ontario. It always intrigues any visitor. It's as if they are transported into a new world where they can relax and enjoy the environment. They get to know us better and our interests. They see our old backyard well that Gary restored – a challenging task. Then they are far more able to show love to us in our time of need when we are hit with a crisis or not.

Pie a la mode, anyone?

Gary's Take

The New Testament mentions hospitality among Christians nine times. Four different writers command hospitality. It is not an option for a loving Christian. It is a requirement to hold the office of "*overseer*" ("*episkopon*") according to 1 Timothy 3:2 and Titus 1:8.

The following is an important aside. "*Episkopon*" ("*overseer*" or "*bishop*") is used six times in the New Testament. Once it refers to Jesus (1 Peter 2:25). In Acts 20:28 it says that the overseers shepherd the flock or the church. Philippians 1:1 distinguishes the "*overseers*" from the "*deacons*." The term overseer is equivalent to the terms "*elder*" ("*presbyterous*") and "*pastor*" ("*poimenas*"). We know this because the term "*pastor*" ("*shepherd*") is only used once in the New Testament referring to leaders in churches. But the activity of shepherding is tied to the work of the "*overseer*." Then the "*elders*" are described as the ones who "*shepherd*" in 1 Peter 5:1-2. The word "*elder*" is used 30 times in describing a class of church leaders. Remember, the word "*pastor*" is only used once. We have no list of requirements attached to "*presbyterous*" or "*poimenas*" but we do have two lists attached to the "*episkopon*." All three positional terms refer to the same leaders. Those leaders have a job qualification of being hospitable. The "*deacons*" don't have that specific requirement. (1 Timothy 3:8-9)

Why is that important?

Leaders lead. Church leaders lead by example. There are various ways of understanding church leadership. However, it is clear that anyone who is described as a "*pastor*", "*elder*" or "*overseer*" must be "*hospitable*." That is because all believers are commanded, *"Be hospitable to one another without complaint."* (1 Peter 4:9) And the pastor must be an example. There is no place for an inhospitable pastor.

I heard that one pastor when moving on from a megachurch gave advice to his successor to live as far away from the church building as he could so the people couldn't find him. Very few people knew where the pastor lived and even fewer had been in his home. Thankfully the new pastor ignored that advice. Obviously in a large church the pastor cannot have everyone to their home. But a person is disqualified from pastoring or eldering if they don't have some people into the home. Circumstances will vary. Marital status and spouses working outside the home will make for a challenge in scheduling and arranging hospitable events. But pastors or elders lead in hospitality.

Hospitality is a developable skill just like preaching. Pastors should invest themselves in both and many other skills as well. The pastor's spouse must grasp that hospitality is part of the job. The job is not something you can leave at the office. The Bible demands that the role expand into the home. There is some modest extra expense involved. You don't need to offer a full meal all the time. Simple fare will serve just as well. People relax more when they have something to eat and drink but you can keep it really simple and still achieve the same end result. Whatever you do, don't try to impress anyone with your culinary skills if you have them. Just make what you offer reasonably pleasing. Wendy has a recipe for apple bread that she has carried with us for over five decades. She got the recipe from a professor's wife at our Bible College. Most of the time there is a loaf of apple bread in our freezer ready to go at a moment's notice. Zap it. Cut it. Plate it. Serve it. Done.

If all are to show hospitality that means all. Poorer people must not be embarrassed about their home. If it has a mud floor sweep it! If the chair works for the poor person it will work for a rich person. If your home isn't perfectly clean don't use that as an excuse to avoid inviting others over. Clean it or accept the imperfection. But don't eliminate hospitality. Hospitality is the gateway to deep relationships. The cumulative requirement in all these "*one anothers*" will fail without hospitality.

Churches can bubble up from the bottom. Church members who excel in hospitality create the loving atmosphere required to move a church forward. When you think about it, you realize that the friends you accumulate over the years are people you have into your home. When you have someone over for tea and toast you notice a qualitative difference in their bond with you the next time you see them. More hospitality leads to more bonding leads to more caring leads to more life change. It's not complicated. Put the coffee pot on.

Your Take

1. When was the last time you had someone over to your house? How did it go?
2. What is your big obstacle in showing more hospitality? Who will help you overcome that?
3. Who comes to mind as someone or some family from your church you need to have to your house soon?

~ 8 ~

Come Together

"... there should be no division in the body, but that its parts should have equal concern for each other." (1 Corinthians 12:25)

We are one. That is easy to say but because we are all so very different it is harder to live out. From the most prominent to the least recognized the people of the church are called to show equal concern for one another. In times of crisis a church may rally around one. The key is to rally around all at all times.

Wendy's Take

So how many funerals have you attended in your life time? Every funeral is different as to how family members honor their loved one that has passed along to eternity. Christian services are definitely different than those held for someone who has not been a follower of Jesus Christ. There doesn't seem to be much hope or joy in the room; however, in the majority of situations equal concern for the grieving family is displayed by all who attend. That may or may not last during the months and years to come. This is the time that a church family must not forget to step up with their love and care nor must they not forget about other grieving families that have also lost dear ones.

Yesterday a middle age pastor friend of ours died. He was so full of energy, nuttiness and a keen desire to see all of his congregation come to know his Savior. Gary and I look forward to him being honored at his funeral. He leaves behind a lovely wife and four children plus many other family members. No doubt, this is a bewildering time for everyone even though his death has been expected for many months. One son asked his mom, "What will we do without Dad?" For sure, many church members will help them through their suffering as they suffer in this loss as well. Paul, the apostle of the New Testament, who wrote to the Corinthian believers, knew the extreme importance of comfort and support in church life equally for everyone whether in a crisis or not.

Gary's Take

It is time for a quick review. You recall there are 63 times in the New Testament where the word "*allélón*" is used to describe the relationships amongst believers. A few of the concepts are repeated but there are well over 30 different elements we are to keep in mind at all times. Some of them have to do with how we talk to each other; some have to do with our attitudes to each other; and yet others speak directly of our actions. Generally speaking, all three – talk, attitude and action – are combined in each reference with one aspect taking the prominent role.

In the case highlighted in this chapter, it is plain to see that all aspects come together as one. Paul speaks of the church with the analogy of the human body. All of our body parts are necessary and must fit together as one. It would create an untenable situation if there was an argument within our brain about whether a finger or toe should be the part to move in a particular direction or do a particular job. You don't walk with your fingers or easily pick up a pencil with your toes. Our body parts are not all designed to do the same actions. Paul rhetorically asks, "*If the whole body were an eye, where would the sense of hearing be? If the whole body were an ear, where would the sense of smell be?*" (1 Corinthians 12:17)

The key to all this working properly is that each part be concerned about every other part. Physically speaking, when one part of your body is out of sorts the other parts compensate for it. When you have a sprained ankle, you limp. You don't think about how to limp; you just do it. Think for a moment of all of the adjustments your body naturally makes to limp temporarily while the one injured part heals. This can only happen if the entire body works as a team.

Isn't it interesting how that analogy is instantly understood as applying to how a group of people must act inside the life of the church?

Thus we can see in Wendy's story how one set of believers is rallying around a family at a time of grief that was expected even though it was a long time coming. But in this case, the members who are deeply hurting are well known because of their prominent role in the church.

But what will happen when some less known person faces similar grief? It is safe to project there may be less help and support expressed. But all the members of the body are to *"have equal concern for each other."* (1 Corinthians 12:25) You might raise the point that everyone may not know the other member and therefore be less inclined to react with support. That is true; but should it be that way?

We get to know about 60 people in our local church. That has been demonstrated over time by several researchers. Therefore, it is possible for one person to show some level of mutual concern for about 59 others in a church. In a large church that may be only 10-20% of the church participants. In a more usual size church that is closer to 100% awareness. (A church with attendance of 60 people normally has about 120 who identify that church as their church home.) Smaller churches are at an advantage here. This actually is a huge advantage if everyone agrees to get to know their 60 acquaintances better. Naturally every individual will know some of their 60 better than others. In a larger church there is the potential of having sub-divisions among the people which make the church more manageable.

It might be helpful to see this with a different analogy than the body. Think for a moment of the church as an orange. There is the whole orange but there are natural divisions within the orange as sections are separated by membranes. A church can organize this way to help fulfill the obligation to have mutual concern within the sections. There are various ways to do this but that is beyond the subject of this book.

From the lowliest to the most prominent there must be a mutual concern and interest for each member. It takes a keen eye and intentionality to notice the concerns of the less obvious people. But they are nonetheless equally important. Don't measure your church by the most visible people or elements; measure it by the way it takes care of the least. The lower income and lower status people are just as important as the wealthy with a pedigree. The opinions of the mentally disadvantaged are as important as the opinions of the highly educated. In final decision making, complicated issues must be considered with a high level of awareness that may not be equally understood by all. However, all concerns must be taken into consideration.

The objective in this verse is that "*there should be no division in the body*." (1 Corinthians 12:25) In fact, the church at Corinth to which Paul spoke was divided in many ways. That will become clear to you if you read the whole letter of 1 Corinthians looking for the evidence of divisiveness.

No church is perfectly unified. But every member of every church should be constantly working for the unity of the church. This can't mean working to get everyone unified around your personal concerns. It does mean everyone looking out for the concerns of all the others.

Your Take

1. Are there times when you wish that others in your church noticed or knew more about your personal struggles and did something about them? Think about how this impacts your relationships in your church.
2. Armed with the knowledge of your own isolation, how can you put your own resolve into action to take care of others who are needing the body?
3. Where could your church organize itself better to exhibit mutual concerns? What are you going to do to become part of the solution?

~ 9 ~

Fellowship

"But if we walk in the light, as he is in the light, we have fellowship with one another, and the blood of Jesus, his Son, purifies us from all sin." (1 John 1:7)

The word "*fellowship*" is used a lot in churches. But surely it is more than coffee and donuts in the church basement. Every time a church gets people together where they can talk to each other we use that word. This deserves more thought.

Wendy's Take

Over the many years in our ministry, Gary and I have learned that starting a new church from scratch is exciting and fulfilling. It is interesting how you can get to try out new ideas – some that turn out great and others not so much. We have just helped a young pastor and his wife start a church in Milton, Ontario. The best idea we have tried is to meet in a restaurant for our Sunday morning service at 10:00 am and then at 11:00 am, when the restaurant opens for the day, we order lunch for everyone. That actually pays for our rent for the location which is cheaper than renting a school. This is looked upon favorably by many a restaurant owner as it helps their bottom line when their business is slow.

More importantly, eating lunch together provides a great time of fellowship for everyone. Young children are not anxiously hoping to get home for something to eat while they impatiently wait for their parents to stop talking. Since there is lots of time for good conversations, we become a church family more quickly, getting to know one another better as we spend more quality time with each other. And any leftover food can be doggy-bagged, particularly for those who do not have much from one week to the next. I was enthralled by the look of surprise and innocence of a seven-year old boy when we all sang Happy Birthday to him one Sunday. In only six month's time, his father has decided to become a follower of Jesus after struggling through all of his life. When you reach out intentionally with the Gospel you never know how God will surprise you by bringing someone around the corner. Quality time spent means quality fellowship resulting in long-lasting, positive repercussions. Now, who wouldn't go for that?

Gary's Take

The Greek word for "*fellowship*" in the New Testament is quite surprisingly not a commonly used word. That is especially true in the sense we use it of connection among people in sharing together. The word is used four times in the first chapter of 1 John. Let's look at that.

"*We proclaim to you what we have seen and heard, so that you also may have fellowship with us. And our fellowship is with the Father and with his Son, Jesus Christ.*" (1 John 1:3) John uses the plural pronouns "*we, us*" and "*our.*" It would appear that John was alone in exile as he wrote this with no local church around him. Yet he sees the grand plural picture of which he is a part. This "fellowship" is said to combine people, "*the Father and his Son, Jesus Christ*" as one. To John this is not mystical because he says unequivocally, "*we have seen with our eyes, which we have looked at and our hands have touched.*" (1 John 1:1) John is not hesitant to talk about his personal engagement with, "*... the Word of life. The life appeared; we have seen it and testify to it, and we proclaim to you the eternal life, which was with the Father and has appeared to us.*" (1 John 1:2) John was compelled to share this message. One could imagine that if he didn't joyfully let it out no matter the cost he would explode!

John's expressiveness tells us something of the well-formed Christian life. It is in vogue to say that faith is a private matter. It is certainly true that belief in Jesus is not made up, plastered on the outside like an actor playing a mime part. This belief is deep in the inner part of true believers. John never uses the noun form of the word for faith. He only uses the verb form which denotes the active, living and life changing commitment every true believer has. This commitment and fellowship saturates the mind and heart.

It is there with you at all times. It sneaks out of your mouth even if you wish you could keep it in. It would be impossible for John to imagine a non-verbal believer.

Lest we fall into the trap of thinking this life is a life of perfect obedience, John introduces another factor. It is the sin factor. We can't properly grasp the phrase "*fellowship with one another*" (1 John 1:7) without understanding the sin issue. Apparently there were hypocrites to be dealt with in the early church. One of the complaints about church life in our century is that churches are full of hypocrites – people pretending they are something they are not. There will always be people in church who pretend to have it all together and don't show any (or many) sinful cracks. Some actually aren't covering up massive flaws; they truly are further down the road of conquering sinful impulses. Others are humbly willing to admit they turn to sin and wish they didn't. When they are with other believers they do much better. And when they are supported by strong relationships with helpful believers outside the church meetings they make progress on their winding path. Every church is a mixed bag.

John is compelled to remind us, "*If we claim to have fellowship with him and yet walk in the darkness, we lie and do not live out the truth.*" (1 John 1:6) There is no room for someone to live a double life claiming "*fellowship with him*" and having a life well-described as a "*walk in the darkness.*" Liar, liar, pants on fire! So this fellowship thing excludes those in the crowd of "*we*" who simply don't have "*fellowship with him.*" They don't have "*fellowship with him*" because they have unconfessed habitual darkness in the inner recesses of their lives. This isn't the day-to-day misfires we all experience; it is a willful holding of a sin that gives Satan a foothold in our lives. On rare but significant occasions we learn of a Christian leader who has been hiding such an island of sin in their life which breaks through the public fog and is revealed into plain view. So the question is, "Did that person truly have '*fellowship with him*' or were they willfully shutting out grace as a habit of life?" Nobody really knows the whole truth but make no mistake about it the old question "*Will not the Judge of all the earth do right?*" (Genesis 18:25) leaves us with assurance that he will do right.

This brings us to a thorny question. Since almost every church has some people who are, and some people who are not walking with him, is it legitimate to call the church a fellowship? Perhaps so if and only if the culture of the church is striving to that fellowship and those who associate with the church but are not living right are clearly out of line and dealt with accordingly. John assumed sin in the church was a reality and told us what to do about it.

How can we know we are not walking in darkness? Start with the "*one anothers*" and evaluate your own personal life. Set the example for all others around you. Keep the truth bubbling up from the bottom by living as pure a discipleship as you know. Then you can integrate all the other directives of the New Covenant. There are over 400 of them. You don't have the time or the psychic or spiritual energy to worry about the other guy until you have a living example of all the commandments under your belt.

Now the question is how are you going to get yourself moving in that direction? You already know. Ingest the Word. Talk to the Lord. Get with His people. Share the light. Declare your commitment before others. And there is one more key thing you may not have in mind. Get yourself a mentor who is further down the discipleship road than yourself. Your will and commitment are absolutely foundational but you will find it hard to live it out if you don't have a wholesome relationship with at least one trusted mentor. Then surround yourself with the systems and the people who will love and support you down that road.

This "*fellowship*" thing with "*one another*" is huge but it isn't about a church barbecue. Such church events are a good start to bring the human connection and create a seedbed out of which love may grow.

The last part of that one another verse is so cleansing! "*But if we walk in the light, as he is in the light, we have fellowship with one another, and the blood of Jesus, his Son, purifies us from all sin.*" (1 John 1:7) Never forget that fellowship in the truest sense runs very deep among cleansed believers who are committed to each other.

Your Take

1. How would you grade your own focus on "*fellowship*" "*in the light*"? How is that a growing part of your life?
2. What investments do you make to deepen the "*fellowship*" in your church?
3. When do you make the time to intentionally draw people into the deeper "*fellowship*" in your church?

~ 10 ~

I'm Devoted to You

"Be devoted to one another in love."
(Romans 12:10)

Devotion takes many forms. As you think about all the possible objects of devotion you will realize that people pick from a myriad of options. Devotion to anything requires that other possible options must be set aside. You get to pick your objects of devotion. The criteria you apply as you make your choices will make all the difference.

Wendy's Take

As we wander through our home we see so many items that have been gifted to us by family or church members expressing their devotion to us in our half century of ministry – pictures, plants, knickknacks, chairs, dining-room suite etc. We even have been given several cars. These hold cherished memories of all those we have worked with in one way or another.

A cone-shaped vase sitting on the shelf of our dining-room buffet was presented to us by a young lady who came to the small group in our home for a short period of time. It came with a cheque that she could ill afford for an airline ticket to Korea. Here is the story. We adopted our youngest son Lee from South Korea when he turned six years old. At this point he was 14 and hoping to return to his old orphanage for a visit but we simply did not have the money for the trip. Our daughter, Lee's sister Sara and husband Chris were in Japan teaching English. They agreed to meet up with Lee in Tokyo and take him back over to Kim Hai, South Korea during their vacation if only we could get him to Tokyo. God was with them all in this interesting adventure but that's another story to tell. That young lady saw the need and generously picked up the cost. She shortly thereafter moved to British Columbia and we lost touch. Apparently through our influence in her life she felt she had gotten her act together spiritually. We haven't heard about her since but her devotion shown through her generosity made a huge impact on our lives as a family.

Gary's Take

Jesus said, "*No one can serve two masters. Either you will hate the one and love the other, or you will be devoted to the one and despise the other. You cannot serve both God and money.*" (Matthew 6:24) The object of devotion will become a master. A master tells you what to do. If you want to follow that master it will impact everything about your time, money, personal development, thoughts and energy. Be careful how you choose.

Serving God is highlighted as the best object of devotion several times throughout the New Testament. That devotion contains several parts. In the early church, "*They devoted themselves to the apostles' teaching and to fellowship, to the breaking of bread and to prayer.*" (Acts 2:42) "*... the household of Stephanas were the first converts in Achaia, and they have devoted themselves to the service of the Lord's people.*" (1 Corinthians 16:15) Notice that the four things mentioned in Acts 2:42 are focused on the things Christians should do when they meet. But the second reference from 1 Corinthians 16:15 seems to refer to the activities of this one household in serving others. By its nature if the one household is centered out as the example, the activity must have been service beyond the collective meetings of the church.

In Canada, on a winter Sunday morning you will find the hockey arenas full of people bundled up holding a Tim Horton's paper cup. They are devoted more to the children and youth they brought to the arena than they are to the game played on the ice. Back in the day there were very few believers in the crowd because they were devoted to the Sunday School instead. Now if you ask someone where they were last Sunday they are likely in regretful yet sanctimonious tones to say they had to (HAD TO) go to a tournament for their child. Devotion. Take your pick.

Somewhere along the line somebody invented the term "family first." That implies that everything else should follow and you get to pick the order. The religious version of that is God first, family second, maybe job third and church last. This is nonsense from a biblical perspective. Jesus was asked about the question of priorities by some smart religious leaders. The question was, "*Teacher, which is the greatest commandment in the Law?*"(Matthew 22:36) Jesus answered the initial question and then answered the implied follow up question as well. *"Jesus replied: 'Love the Lord your God with all your heart and with all your soul and with all your mind.' This is the first and greatest commandment. And the second is like it: 'Love your neighbor as yourself.' All the Law and the Prophets hang on these two commandments.*" (Matthew 22:37-38) Even the sanctimonious Pharisees missed the opportunity. If they had it in mind they could have asked. "And where should the family fit in?" They didn't. To a similar query recorded in Luke 10:25-37 Jesus gave the story we call The Good Samaritan. This answered the question about neighbors. Again, no mention of family time. Rather this was all about sacrificial service time.

It is a common thread for a rebellious child to complain that their family was too religious and they didn't get to have any fun. Life was boring, and restricted so they say. Interestingly, children from the same home who follow the Lord seldom have recollection of this imprisoned and deprived life. When parents follow the Lord, of course they are devoted to their children and give them a wide range of life opportunities. It is just that the opportunities differ from their non Christian friends. God designed the world so that we could have life to the max. Jesus himself said, "T*he thief comes only to steal and kill and destroy; I have come that they may have life, and have it to the full.*" (John 10:10) Robbing a child of good Sabbath experience is thievery.

"*Observe the Sabbath day by keeping it holy, as the Lord your God has commanded you.*" (Deuteronomy 5:12) Sprinkled throughout the Old Testament there are references to this imperative. That carries over into the New Testament as a principle but the day migrated from the Sabbath (seventh) Day to the First Day. See Acts 20:7. I really love the one day in seven principle and that we now emphasize the first day. This isn't about rest at the end of a grueling week; it is all about rest at the beginning of a hopeful coming week to serve the Lord.

This isn't controversial in the Lord's eyes. He expects you to hit the reset button on Sunday with devotion to the things of God and the people of God. If you can't fit your hobby or recreational pursuit into another day then find a different pursuit. As J. B. Phillips paraphrased, "*With eyes wide open to the mercies of God, I beg you, my brothers, as an act of intelligent worship, to give him your bodies, as a living sacrifice, consecrated to him and acceptable by him. Don't let the world around you squeeze you into its own mould, but let God re-mould your minds from within, so that you may prove in practice that the plan of God for you is good, meets all his demands and moves towards the goal of true maturity."* (Romans 12:1-2)

When Christians allow anything to squeeze out their devotion to "*one another*" they fail. Sunday isn't a day for finishing up last week's failed chores.

Your Take

1. Was there a day when you were more devoted to God's people? If so, what happened to allow the sacrifice to get dusty and unpolished?
2. What should you cut back on in order to heighten your devotion to others in your church?
3. Have you let the lack of devotion by others get you down? Why would you let their problem become your problem?

~ 11 ~

After You

"Honor one another above yourselves."
(Romans 12:10)

Honor is respect we usually reserve for people of high estate or value. But the New Testament applies the concept to the full spectrum of people. Someone might not honor you but you don't have to live down to their standard. Let's think about that.

Wendy's Take

A friend of ours started attending a different church in her community. After four months of attendance she happened to notice that the sign above the Welcome Center had been placed way too high for anyone to notice it. She recommended that the sign be lowered to a pastoral staff member who thought that would be a good idea. However, five years later the sign is still flying high. Either the pastor had forgotten about her suggestion or didn't think it was important enough to do anything about it.

Good ideas of improvement can get lost in the busyness of church life. And how does that person feel about their suggestion being ignored today? Even though this was a minor detail that was overlooked, it shows a lack of respect for this person who probably does not want to mention it again or make any more insightful suggestions. The church loses when a person comes along who has developed church expertise in their past that could be of great benefit in a new situation but is ignored. All ideas need to be valued when presented or discarded with good reasons as to why they cannot be implemented if that is the case. The Apostle Paul believed that honoring each one in the church was an important issue. (Romans 12:10)

Gary's Take

It is safe to say that everyone wants to be worthwhile and at the same time it would be nice to feel worthwhile and appreciated. Life is a grind. And in the dailyness of grinding it out, it is hard to see the end from the beginning. After all, today is a beginning. Everything that has passed is past. But it is not that simple because everything from the past is hanging around in each head as noise.

Satan loves to amplify that noise. He is described as *"... the accuser of our brothers and sisters"* (Revelation 12:10); but bear in mind that this prophetic passage speaks to his ultimate defeat. He keeps yapping at God about how much of a failure you are – me too. How is one to have a sense of being worthwhile with all that noise? Satan's defeat is sure but not yet complete. Our personal salvation is sure but not yet complete as well. We have an interim remedy for our own failure. It is the forgiveness of God. *"If we confess our sins, he is faithful and just and will forgive us our sins and purify us from all unrighteousness."* (1 John 1:9) What a deal! We confess; he forgives. Move on and become even more worthwhile.

That is why we need to pay special attention to how we treat each other. We don't need another place or person to tell us how much we mess up. We know; we already know. But we do need regular reminders that *"God's love has been poured out into our hearts through the Holy Spirit"* (Romans 5:5) and that the Lord's words to Paul apply to us, *"My grace is sufficient for you, for my power is made perfect in weakness."* (2 Corinthians 12:9)

A great place to start to rehabilitate each other is to honor each other as the wonderful recipients of the grace and love that we are. When a baby takes first steps we honor that child with looks of affirmation, clapping of hands and squeals of joy – so much so that the child is so distracted by our fuss and falls. We don't scold. We share the loss and encourage the child to try again. We honor that child; we honor the effort.

The Bible says, *"... honor your father and mother"* in both the Old and New Testaments. Twenty times in the Proverbs we are given sage advice about honor. Look it up. Ultimate honor belongs to the Father and the Son.

You can't have one without the other. (John 5:23) This is all a backdrop to Paul's simple statement that we are to *"honor one another."* (Romans 12:10)

From the most prominent member to the lowliest we all need to know we are worthwhile. If the others around you don't hear it from your lips they may never hear it at all. You honor someone when you show appreciation for how they lived in an exact moment; how they behaved under certain stimuli or stress and how that makes you feel personally. That person may not even know they did what they did. But if you noticed something good, honor it and the person. Nobody naturally notices when things go smoothly but they certainly do when things go wrong. You can notice and honor the good. For example, you can be the one to commend a father or mother for disciplining a child in a firm but respectful way. Wait a week before you tell that person and the impact will be even greater.

Imagine for a moment how the mood in your church would be lifted if as a matter of sincere habit even 10% of the ardent members developed the intentional habit of first of all noticing and then secondly commenting on things that deserve honor. Can you feel the difference? Can you see the pride on the face of the teenager when some adult they barely know compliments them on their work at school, sports or church? Can you imagine the satisfaction in that mentally disadvantaged member who picks up stray papers on the church floor when you comment on how much you appreciate the job they regularly do? How about those who lead at the front of meetings? What about that shy child who sings in the church band for the first time? Did you notice the courage that took? Perhaps someone gave a testimony for the first time, or prayed in public, or just simply started to arrive earlier. Did you notice? Did you give them honor where honor was due?

When you do give that honor, look the person straight in the eye as you speak. Move in just a little closer. Perhaps put a hand on a shoulder or hold that handshake just a little longer. By your demeanor and tone of voice show your sincere appreciation.

And don't forget those who are in charge. *"Have confidence in your leaders and submit to their authority, because they keep watch over you as those who must give an account. Do this so that their work will be a joy, not a burden, for that would be of no benefit to you."* (Hebrews 13:17)

A church full of people who genuinely honor one another is a wonderful, positive uplifting place. It is something you can do. No, it is something you must do if you are living in obedience to the Savior.

Your Take

1. Can you recall the last time you showed honor where it was due? In addition to the sensations in your consciousness, how did you show that honor outwardly?
2. Do you see your failure to honor another as the sin it is? Have you confessed it and received forgiveness?
3. What will you do this week to look for places to honor other fellow pilgrims in your church?

~ 12 ~

I Prayed for You

"Pray for each other so that you may be healed." (James 5:16)

A form of prayer comes naturally but not the real prayer that makes a difference. Much prayer is really just wishing for what the person wants and begging some god to supply the lack. However, genuine prayer, when you know the One to whom you pray, moves the hand of God and changes the hearts of people.

Wendy's Take

How often have you heard the promise, "I will remember to pray for you"? My next question is how do you know that person will actually remember to pray? You can be sure they will pray for you if you hear them pray out loud in your presence.

A few years ago Gary and I were involved in a small group. One of the women who had come from an abusive background was too afraid or maybe too stubborn to pray out loud. Gary suggested that she pray just a few words as if Jesus were sitting in the empty chair in the room. I guess that helped for she did take the challenge and it was so encouraging and refreshing for the rest of us to hear her faltering words. We all exclaimed "yes!" when she finished. It is hard to imagine that later down the road she took on the leadership of that small group. She was not without her weaknesses but from that experience her confidence seemed to soar within herself. Last year she met her Maker when she died of cancer. I'm sure He commended her on her willingness to try and change.

Why is it that many Christians are afraid to pray out loud? When that person is led to Christ to become His follower initially how often is there a lack of training so that they can realize how important it is to learn to pray out loud for others? This step of obedience is one in many that will help to build confidence in their spiritual walk and be a wonderful inspiration to those who hear their simple, honest talk with Jesus.

Gary's Take

James is the one who says, *"... pray for each other."* (James 5:16) No other New Testament writer ties prayer to the term "*one another.*" And James uses a different word for prayer than the usual. However, before we think about what James says, here are a few observations.

Jesus saturated his days with prayer. The perfect God-Man invested time in prayer. When he did so the Gospels record that he often prayed by himself. He went away to the mountains. He got up before the others around him. Prayer needs solitude. *"But Jesus often withdrew to lonely places and prayed."* (Luke 5:16) He didn't instruct us to do that directly but he set the example we would do well to follow. On several occasions he taught, *"When you pray ..."* because he knew we would.

This isn't a book about prayer; it is a book about the Christian's responsibility to others – especially other believers. That includes prayer. The Bible is full of instruction on prayer and everyone would be wise to figure out what prayer is supposed to be about. Make that a lifelong concern. One thing is certain. Prayer is not for a whiny child of God to beg for what he wants to make his life more comfortable or to gain more praise for himself.

In a list of bullet points Paul commands this, *"Rejoice always, pray continually, give thanks in all circumstances; for this is God's will for you in Christ Jesus."* (1 Thessalonians 5:16-18) These elements all link together as parts of God's will for your life. Since you care to know God's will for your life start right here. Don't over complicate it. The Lord is interested in who you are much more than where you are in terms of your job, your geographical location including your country.

Knowing God's will takes a prior commitment to doing his will. This isn't something you shop for as if it is a new piece of clothing for you to try on. You take care of who you are and let the Lord take care of where you are. He will guide your steps when you let him. Decide now to start with a life that is saturated with continual rejoicing, prayer and thanksgiving. Those elements of life are based on choices you make, not something circumstances give to you. Perfect circumstances are an illusion. Striving to be a perfect person is not optional. *"Be perfect, therefore, as your heavenly Father is perfect."* (Matthew 5:48) Think of perfect as being the exact person you were meant to be. That would mean that the real life you live is perfectly in sync with the ideal life you were designed to live.

Now back to James. The whole verse is, *"Therefore confess your sins to each other and pray for each other so that you may be healed. The prayer of a righteous person is powerful and effective."* (James 5:16) You will immediately notice that he uses the term for *"each other"* or *"one another"* twice in one verse. Generally, James is very personal and hard hitting in his writings.

Here you can feel personal intimacy more than in-your-face directives. If you simply take the one phrase *"... pray for each other so that you may be healed"* (James 5:16) and think about it, you will feel the personal connection James encourages. He anticipates healing if people engage in prayer about their ailments. However, it seems James was more concerned about the inner healing of the soul than the healing of the body. He gives us that clue in the preceding admonishment to confess our sins to each other. Do you see a prayer meeting here with several participants or two people opening their hearts to one another?

I don't think a week goes by when I don't have a heart-to-heart conversation with one or more individuals where that person shares something with me that they have never talked about with anyone else. Sometimes it is a story of long ago when the person experienced some deep hurt. Sometimes it is a wish or desire for life going forward. Often these conversations give me plenty to pray about when I am alone. I find that when my friends share their burdens they are comforted. I avoid trying to find answers for their troubles and just share my own concern for them, desiring that the Lord will once again heal circumstances.

If you don't talk to other believers personally and allow the conversation to set down roots into the heart, you will miss out on one of life's great blessings. It is a good idea to pray with each other. It is more essential to pray for each other. And it is a special blessing to hear others pray in your presence. Make it your habit to get your head out of your own troubles and into the troubles of others. Bless others with your prayers in groups and in your own quiet places. James promises, *"The prayer of a righteous person is powerful and effective."* (James 5:16)

Your Take

1. Do you invest your prayers in others much more than upon your own needs? How can you work at becoming better at that?
2. When do you bless others by enthusiastically praying in groups? If not, have you shared your reluctance with others to enlist their encouragement?
3. How much time do you actually invest in praying? Is it enough?

~ 13 ~

I Admit It

"Therefore confess your sins to each other ..."
(James 5:16)

When something is an embarrassing goof-up most people find it uncomfortable to let others know. But we all goof. The worst kind of mess up occurs when we choose to do something that is actually sinful. Behind the well-groomed image we like to portray there are always mistakes and worse.

Wendy's Take

I must confess that I have a hard time with mornings. It takes a while for my mind and body to "get up and get at 'em!" With my quiet nature words are even more scarce at that time of day. Gary will often tease me at the breakfast table, "Do you have anything more to say on that subject?"

When our children were growing up, so that they wouldn't be late for school, I did manage to charge into their dark rooms, lift the blinds on the windows and sing to wake them up, "Let the merry sunshine in, Open up the windows, Open up the doors, Let the merry sunshine in." Maybe I should take my own advice from way back when to create a cheerier atmosphere each new day.

Maybe I should follow through on my wobbly intention to start drinking coffee in the morning since I am Finnish and Fins love their coffee. A jolt of java once a day may help the cause and they say it is supposed to be good for you.

Or maybe I also need to confess that my quietness is partly due to laziness; although I do like to listen more than talk. Am I too lazy to converse much in the morning? Am I too lazy to fight my way into an energized conversation to contribute some meaningful thoughts? I am sure you would concur that it is a challenge to look deeper into your soul – answering tough questions to gain better solutions for treating your varied weaknesses. I am glad the Holy Spirit is around to nudge us along that journey.

Gary's Take

I find the book of James to be an in-your-face challenge. James was a half-brother of Jesus born to Mary and Joseph along with three other brothers and at least two sisters. I wonder what it was like to live with a perfect older brother. (By the way, some don't accept the natural explanation of Mark 6:3 and Matthew 13:55-56 because they seem to want to defend the concept that Mary was a perpetual virgin. But Matthew 1:25 tells us directly that Mary and Joseph had sex after Jesus was born.) They must have had a normal family life except for the perfect older brother. The Bible doesn't tell us anything about those interrelationships. Many believe that James didn't accept the Gospel until after the resurrection. My guess is that is probably true.

But James did lead in the early church and had some strong things to say. He saw the light and was outspoken about its implications. James was for transparency in the church. He doesn't draw attention to the accepted fact that believers need to confess their sins to God. The need for that is clear. See 1 John 1:7-10. But James tells us this isn't just between us and God.

The paragraph in which James says, *"Confess your sins to each other"* contains other admonitions that point to the troubles of life and the need to make those matters known in the church. Personal troubles are a matter for the church, for prayers and for engagement. In addition, when things go well it is something to sing about together. Read that in James 5:13-20.

Christianity is not a private matter, that is, not only a private matter. In our day, it is common for people to hold to the tenet that "everything is just between me and God if I want it that way." Nope. Not true. We don't get it if we think otherwise. All these *"one anothers"* destroy that notion.

I don't believe James is telling us to openly share everything with everybody in a public context. But he also isn't saying confess your sins to any one special person as if that person could give absolution. The emphasis

James has here is intended for all believers to live a life of openness with "*one another.*"

Back in the 19th century a village pastor said farewell to his church and packed up to take a post in a much larger church in the big city. Then he and his wife decided they couldn't do it and returned to the lowlier place for the rest of heir lives. He wrote these words, "Blest be the tie that binds … We share our mutual woes, Our mutual burdens bear; And often for each other flows The sympathizing tear." Google for the whole lyrics and tune if you aren't familiar with the hymn. In that short classic hymn he captures the spirit of James.

Church is messy. People squabble. Christians don't always get it right. I am dumbfounded that people think it will be otherwise. What should be isn't what will be. In the church you are going to sin sometimes and others are going to offend you. But there are *"one another"* remedies. Lots of them. When we apply these humble remedies we create a rich church life. When we don't, we suffer isolation. Our relationships in church aren't characterized by perfection. Putting on a face doesn't cut it. Finding the correct contexts to share personal failings and feelings in the church is a prayerful pursuit. There won't be, nor should there be, much space in the larger meetings for people to have the catharsis of spilling their guts in front of others. Where that happens there is bound to be misunderstanding. You will find that over time others may use what you confess publicly against you.

Every confession of sin should contribute to the person's growth and benefit, not provide a club to beat someone down. It is best to think in terms of confessing faults and propensities much more than describing particular events. Over disclosure won't help build your life or anyone else's.

Pretention is common in church. How about in you? There are parts of your life that remain – and should remain – private. But if you had to put a percentage ratio of how much about what people see of you is real and how much is pretend what would that ratio be? If you are pretending with maybe 20% of what you truly are then you have a lot of work to do on yourself. All may be in equilibrium to the outside world but if you have private garbage you have to get rid of it. If there are some things you need to confess with an "accountablilbuddy" to help you get beyond the chains that bind you, then get to it. If you don't deal with it you might become a casualty by the side of the road. You have seen that, have you not? Someone looks like the real deal and then private sin bursts into the open and others are shocked. Find someone to confess it to with the purpose of overcoming. That is what James would tell you to do.

Your Take

1. Is there something dragging you down? Have you found the right person(s) in your church to share that with so that you can move on?
2. Do others trust you with their private stories so you can help them climb higher? If not, why not?
3. How could others see that you look for the times and the places to help others be transparent and open with you so that you can help them walk as they should?

Push It!

These are some of the things that take some concentration, work and decision making. There is likely nobody looking over your shoulder on these points on a day by-day basis. This isn't like a parent reminding a child to brush their teeth. If there aren't reminders the child might forget. In this case, you must be the adult and make the decisions for yourself or you might slip into negative habits and forget these essentials.

~ 14 ~

I'm for Unity

"... so in Christ we, though many, form one body, and each member belongs to all the others."
(Romans 12:5, also Romans 15:5, Ephesians 4:25)

Countries seldom achieve a high level of unity. Elections are won by the slimmest of margins. We have come to accept political spin as inevitable. Some just throw their hands up in despair. The church has to be different. We need a different set of rules to live by to perpetuate our oneness.

Wendy's Take

How interesting it is that God has created some species of birds that flock together such as geese, crows and sparrows. They all have to be in the same spot. The sparrows enjoy our seed station outside our kitchen window. Often there are 30 of them pecking away at one time. It amazes Gary and me that in a moment for whatever reason they fly to the nearby cedar trees without banging into each in precision formation. One brave soul might be left standing but when that guy leaves another lands on the board by himself, soon to be immediately followed by his friends. They cannot live without each other.

God has created humans to be part of a flock as well; whether it is the family, a sports club, a music group or the church. There is the innate desire for each of us to want to belong to a group.

In the church many an elderly person can look upon their last 50 years of participating in a local assembly and beam with pride when they talk about the church which they have belonged to since childhood. Their church friends have become vital to them in their own development over the years. They have also learned to realize that God knows what's best for his creations.

It is important to you to want to join us perched high upon an electrical wire with close friends nearby to better view, understand and eventually help the world as it passes by. That only happens when the individuals understand how to work together.

Gary's Take

There is an old verse of uncertain origin that goes something like this.

To live above with saints we love,
Oh that will be glory!
To live below with saints we know,
Now that's another story.

In theory most believers accept the concept that we are one. Paul said, "*So in Christ we, though many, form one body, and each member belongs to all the others.*" (Romans 12:5) However, we are also all different. It is the differences that are like boulders on our path together. It is easy to wish everyone would think the same way we do, but they don't. That is where our road together gets rough.

It helps when we realize where our differences come from.

We are at different stages of life. Some have the perspective of youth and others that of older age. Both perspectives are neither good nor bad in and of themselves. However, both can contain faulty elements that need to be corrected.

In growth terms we are all at different levels of maturity when it comes to overcoming our sin nature.

In our new nature we all have different gifting. "*We have different gifts, according to the grace given to each of us.*" (Romans 12:6)

In our natural humanity we are wired different. There are a bevy of theories about our differences. Some have been validated by science but many others have not. Some are useful (or some less useful) constructs developed by those who ponder human nature but the science oriented types turn their nose up at them. I have my favorites in both categories. Others I am not so sure about.

What I am sure about is that we can't be so sure that all we think about our categorizations of humans are valid unless they are solidly based on divine revelation through the Bible.

Even at that, there are various theological perspectives all claiming to be based on the Bible but with significant differences.

None of us will ever get a large body of people who agree with us in every way. We must learn to live with that.

There are a few things we need to build into our foundations. One is simply this, "*Therefore each of you must put off falsehood and speak truthfully to your neighbor, for we are all members of one body.*" (Ephesians 4:25) A commitment to telling the truth is essential. That doesn't mean we are obliged to dump all that is true all at once on everyone. It does mean that there is never space to lead people in the wrong direction with our words.

Another important fact is that a good attitude towards others is something that comes from the Lord. Thus Paul prays, "*May the God who gives endurance and encouragement give you the same attitude of mind toward each other that Christ Jesus had, so that with one mind and one voice you may glorify the God and Father of our Lord Jesus Christ.*" (Romans 15:5-6) What was this Christ-like attitude? Paul just told us, "*We who are strong ought to bear with the failings of the weak and not to please ourselves. Each of us should please our neighbors for their good, to build them up. For even Christ did not please himself but, as it is written: 'The insults of those who insult you have fallen on me.' For everything that was written in the past was written to teach us, so that through the endurance taught in the Scriptures and the encouragement they provide we might have hope.*" (Romans 15:1-4) There is no place for retaliatory words in a Christian's vocabulary.

Unity is elusive in most churches. Fuel burns between and among people with different perspectives all too easily. Every perspective that is consistent with the Word of God must be respected. Sometimes each of us must set aside our personal preferences and just get on with the task of building unity with "one another." When you reflect upon past decisions in your church you are likely to see that many of the disagreements of yesterday often fade into insignificance.

Make it your objective to look at the differences you find from the correct viewpoint. "*Be completely humble and gentle; be patient, bearing with one another in love. Make every effort to keep the unity of the Spirit through the bond of peace.*" (Ephesians 4:2-3)

Your Take

1. Describe a church decision from a while back which at the time was controversial but today seems inconsequential? How could the decision have been processed in a more unified way?
2. Do you recognize in yourself the desire to ignore some facts and emphasize others just to get your own way? If so, how will you give more respect to other viewpoints in the future?
3. What will you do to make sure you are treating everyone in your church with the right attitude? Who can help you see when you are off base? Will you accept a loving rebuke from that person?

~ 15 ~

It's Good for You

"Make sure that nobody pays back wrong for wrong, but always strive to do what is good for each other and for everyone else."
(1 Thessalonians 5:15)

Strangely, doing good gets a bad rap sometimes. That is because some people think they can attain salvation by what they do. No. One only gains salvation by putting their trust in Christ alone for their salvation. They subsequently demonstrate that faith is real by being immersed, obeying the commandments endorsed by Jesus and living out the "one anothers." That includes doing good – not just being a do-gooder.

Wendy's Take

Doesn't it warm your heart when you see a preschooler wanting to share his cookie with his friend or letting his friend lick his lollipop (maybe not so good!)? Most people want what is good for a family member, friend from church or work, neighbor, even a stranger. Many a missionary, even though enduring great hardship, has traveled overseas to a country where the inhabitants have never heard about Jesus' Gospel of hope. The missionaries knew beforehand that this message would be good for their lives.

Women in churches like parties. We have wedding showers, baby showers, birthday/anniversary celebrations. When the last piece of cake has been eaten and everyone has gone home, the recipient of all the attention feels good. They know they are genuinely loved by their church family and have been given a boost in life with all the gifts bestowed upon them. When

Gary and I were first married, the church we were serving in gave us a pantry shower. We were so pleased as our budget those days was being stretched to its limit (not much different today – lol!) in setting up our new household. The people of the church saw in advance what would be good for us. The cost of baking ingredients, paper products, cleaning supplies can really add up. In turn, these people were pleased with themselves as they realized we were pleasantly surprised with their good work.

Cake anyone or should it be a veggie tray?

Gary's Take

Medical doctors traditionally take an oath derived from the original Hypocratic Oath which was written a few centuries before Christ. It doesn't contain the phrase "First do no harm" as is popularly thought but that is the sentiment of the physician's oath.

Many in society take the position that if they don't bother anyone they are living as they should. They don't break and enter, beat people up, exhibit road rage, lie or cheat much so they think they are on a smooth road to the next life if there is a next life. No matter how many sins they live with, as long at they are far enough ahead of enough other people they think they will make it. They somehow got the impression that God distributes salvation like a school where most people pass to the next grade. I hope you know that's not the way it works because "... *all have sinned and fall short of the glory of God* ..." (Romans 3:23) and "*For the wages of sin is death, but the gift of God is eternal life in Christ Jesus our Lord.*" (Romans 6:23)

Some Christians take the unstudied view that as long as they don't harm others they are doing well. But that is not what the Bible says.

Our target verse explains our responsibility clearly. It says, "... *always strive to do what is good for each other and for everyone else.*" (1 Thessalonians 5:15) It is to be every believer's perpetual striving to do good for "*one another.*" That speaks to the insiders in the church. Then Paul adds the phrase, "*...and to everyone else.*" Presumably that is a reference to unbelievers as well. It isn't enough defensively to say, "What? I'm not hurting anyone. It is my own business so get out of my way." Paul said, "*For the grace of God has appeared that offers salvation to all people. It teaches us to say 'No' to ungodliness and worldly passions, and to live self-controlled, upright and godly lives in this present age, while we wait for the blessed* *hope—the appearing of the glory of our great God and Savior, Jesus Christ, who gave himself for us to redeem us from all wickedness and to purify for himself a people that are his very own, eager to do what is good."* (Titus 2:11-14) Our calling is clear; we are a waiting people who in the meantime are eager to do what is good.

As you think about what it is to do good, do you draw a blank? At any given moment that may be so. None of us will have a clue about the good we could be achieving if we don't take some steps. We need to poke around to find out what needs to be done. Then we have to think about when we are going to fit it in. We will have to say "no" to other more comfortable options and put it on our calendar – whatever it is.

I am an advocate for investing five minutes a day in good activities to get habits started. Maybe the good is as simple as bringing in garbage cans for a neighbor who could use a little help. That is one of those little five minute commitments. You can think of a hundred possibilities like that. Doing good must start at home but it needs to break out into other people's lives as well. Why not make it your aim to do something every day? The Boy Scouts official slogan is, "Do a Good Turn Daily." That is an interesting use of the word "turn" but you get the idea.

Include in your thoughts the possibilities of doing good over and over. God built a one-day-in-seven pattern into creation. Good things that you do on a weekly basis make a big difference. You can call someone on the phone weekly or visit together in a home or coffee shop. If everyone in your church had two or three people they ministered to every week what a difference it would make. The point of Bubble UP Church is that you don't need permission to live out the "*one anothers.*" You don't need a church program to make the "one anothers" happen. You can do good just because you do good.

While you are at it become a referee for others to "*Make sure that nobody pays back wrong for wrong ...*" (1 Thessalonians 5:15) Just imagine a church without any kind of retaliation in word or deeds. Imagine a church where everyone does good just because they love Jesus. Let that work start by your example.

Your Take

1. What could you do every week (or on a regular repeated basis) that over

time would be a great bonding experience between you and someone else in your church?

2. Can you make a list of three people you could do good for right now? Will you schedule that good and set it up in your calendar?
3. Who can you become an "accountabilibuddy" for to assure they will do something good and in turn they will see to it that you maintain the do good habit?

~ 16 ~

I'll Encourage You

"Therefore encourage one another and build up one another, just as you also are doing."
(1 Thessalonians 5:11, also 1 Thessalonians 4:18, Hebrews 3:13, 10:25)

How many people believe they get enough encouragement in life? How many people believe they have enough friends who actually and practically care for them? We think you will agree that far too few people think enough people care about them.

Wendy's Take

"So how are you feeling today, Wendy?" Sam sincerely asked me one Sunday after our morning church service. "You look a bit tired." I agreed with him; however, his concern did pick me up which encouraged me for I knew this middle-aged single man had attended our new church start quite faithfully over the previous six months. He came carrying a knapsack of troubles that weighed heavily on his back which included a young son with autism and an older son with his own set of health issues. Our pastor's wife had invited him to church, a place he had never been before, after meeting him at a local restaurant where they served together. He came looking for answers.

Since his first visit Gary has been meeting weekly with Sam for about an hour. He has become Sam's answer man, it seems, for even though he is not a young man, he still has a lot to learn about day-to-day living and how many of his problems can be helped through Jesus Christ. What is really encouraging is that he is teachable and willing to put into practice suggestions given. Every week that goes by we see noticeable changes. He is even sleeping better at night and he doesn't have as many headaches – both a big plus. If for no one else, our church start is worth it for Sam, his family members and others he is bringing out who are falling more and more in love with Jesus.

Whenever Gary and I need some encouragement we can think of Sam. Not all the rough edges are gone but the growth is amazing. There is nothing that encourages us more than watching people like Sam make significant progress in their lives.

Gary's Take

I heard a TV preacher yesterday tell of a time when a neighbor across his back fence was in deep trouble and he thought he should speak to him but he didn't know how to begin. Later that man died and the chaplain from the hospital called the TV preacher to tell him of the passing. The preacher explained that he had never talked to the man but appreciated the call. The chaplain's response was that the man had watched him regularly on television and so thought they had an active relationship. The preacher expressed regret that he had failed this man. It's too easy for us all to think the other person doesn't need our encouragement but we surely could use theirs.

Encouragement comes in different shapes. There are simple things we can do to encourage others by helping them with a project, giving a gift, sending a card, email or text. However, the most encouraging initiative we can take is to use audible words. The voice can convey our personality better than written words ever can, however, there is certainly a time for written words. Many people feel they can be more precise with written words. What we write has the advantage that the words may be read over and over. But then if the words don't convey the meaning we intended, written words may also amplify a negative message. Spoken words over the telephone allow for more conveyance of emphasis and emotions to get our message across. Adding the visual component with video chat creates another helpful layer for meaning exchange. But face-to-face is better yet. After all is said and done conveying an encouraging meaning exchange is what encouragement is all about.

Paul gives us some important fine-tuning for our encouraging activities in 1 Thessalonians 5:14 when he says "*And we urge you, brothers and sisters, warn those who are idle and disruptive, encourage the disheartened, help the weak, be patient with everyone."* The main characteristic with which we must treat everyone is patience. But within that patient approach we should use words of warning with lazy people in the church. We should encourage the disheartened. There are always disheartened people around us who could use some encouraging words. But sometimes encouragement must take a more practical turn when we help people who are simply too weak to help themselves.

Years ago a very good friend of mine was sent reeling after his wife left him, took the children and eventually divorced him. I was sitting with my friend in his home when another friend came to visit. That visit was really appreciated. The other man noticed the dirty dishes piled high in the sink spilling over onto the counter. He said to my hurting friend, "When you finish using a cup why don't you simply rinse it out and put it back in the cupboard?" I remember my friend's response very well. He said, "That is a simple concept but I just can't do it." He needed help not instruction. The encouragement would have been far stronger if the second man had said to me, "Gary, come and help me wash up these dishes."

In 1 Thessalonians Paul says *"encourage one another"* twice. (1 Thessalonians 4:18, 5:11) He talks about the encouragement of words about the second coming. Then in the second reference he adds the observation that they are already doing this.

It is safe to say that if we as individuals don't intentionally think about how we can encourage others we won't do it as often as we should because we just won't think of it often enough. If we don't think in advance we will be left with spur of the moment opportunities only. And don't forget how encouraging it is to remind others that Jesus is coming back and all the unfairness will be set aside by the Prince of Peace.

If Paul wrote to your church with a reminder could he say, *"Therefore encourage one another and build each other up, just as in fact you are doing."*? (1 Thessalonians 5:11) Is it happening around you?

Your Take

1. What was the most encouraging action or words that someone in your church gave to you in the past month? Do you see how important that was to you?

2. Who do you know who needs encouraging right now? How will you overcome your feeling that you don't know how to supply encouragement and just do or say something today?
3. By being the encourager in your sphere of connections at church how will that improve the atmosphere?

~ 17 ~

Poke Me

"Let us consider how to stimulate one another to love and good deeds." (Hebrews 10:24)

Sometimes teenagers need a poke to get them started in the morning. They stay up too late and wonder why they are so sleepy in the morning. Isn't that interesting? Most of us need a poke once in a while because we don't see the cause and effect bond. We need others to remind us and get us going again.

Wendy's Take

I have been tricking my husband all summer. We have a small two-storey out building in our backyard – downstairs is his workshop and upstairs his office. I have been de-cluttering the mess in both places that has accumulated far too long. This building has been a great space to stash renovation materials from ongoing projects in our main house along with multiple computer parts such as oodles of wires (I thought this was to be a wireless society!) To keep from bugging him with all my questions as to what items he wants to keep I have brought a small box of stuff into our kitchen and put it on the counter day after day. At supper time he will quickly peruse it all and create a garbage pile. This appeases me with my philosophy of use it or get rid of it. Very often he will even find a treasure he had been missing. My second philosophy is if you have a huge task to conquer, do a little each day and pretty soon you will find that the task is complete. This process is also a benefit for our children who will have to deal with our estate after we have passed on to Glory.

Gary has his own philosophy; if a task will only take five minutes to finish, do it right then and there instead of taking time to add it to the "to do" list. You probably won't be able to find that list any way! We are both slowly spurring each other to do what is good even though it may just be inconsequential de-cluttering. And that's Biblical according to Hebrews 10:24, right? This is something that needs to be taught to all procrastinators so that more can be accomplished in their own lives and others.

Gary's Take

"Live and let live" simply doesn't work to build a better world. Tolerance and acceptance are admirable qualities only when they are matched with encouragement to always do better. Many people known for their greatness had only their inner drive for improvement to take them to a level of attainment nobody else expected. But they are the exception. Most of us desperately need someone to believe in us before we put out the effort to improve.

The writer of Hebrews understood this. That is why he said we have to think about it. We are required "*to stimulate one another*." (Hebrews 10:24) That is not about making suggestions. The word translated "*stimulate*" is a strong word. It means, "incitement, irritation, stimulation and provocation." It is often used in the negative sense of picking a fight. Therefore, our job with each other is to take the initiative to poke each other. The poking is to get more love and more good deeds out of each other.

The great exhibition in love is in good deeds, not in warm fuzzy emotions. When you get poked you don't appreciate it at first. But when it is a good poke and you respond positively you achieve at a level you never thought possible.

This is another tricky business for us all. If you are not careful what you intend as a stimulation to good may be taken as a scolding. Shame is one of the strong human emotions. We all know we mess up way too much. When we do and someone scolds us for it we feel discouraged.

Some would say we don't want to lay a guilt trip on people. Uh, not exactly. When we are guilty we need someone to help us face it. Guilt is a great motivator. It is false guilt that tears us down. When someone uses words and actions to attempt to make us feel guilty when we are not, it is abuse. It is that abuse we must avoid. However, calling someone out for inferior behavior when the behavior or attitude is inferior isn't abusive when it is done in the right way and with love.

Simulating someone in the right direction needs to start with a private conversation. If that conversation isn't heeded it is time to repeat the conversation with a few other witnesses who agree on the assessment. Eventually it may become a public rebuke. But not often.

Such conversations need to start with what you don't want to have happen. You always need to explain what a negative outcome would be and point to the positive outcome you are longing for. You don't want to put people down; you want to build them up. Tell them so. You don't want them to feel rejected and discouraged; you want to generate hope and encouragement. Tell them so. You don't want to misunderstand what is going on in their lives. There may be factors at play you didn't know. Low performance could come from past hurts or present debilitating factors you don't know about. Make sure you do your best to understand and give opportunity for explanation and discussion. Make every effort to work toward successful conclusions where you participate as a helper, not a judge.

It is difficult when the person you are confronting seems to be responsive during the conversation and the result seems positive only to find out later the conversation created pain without remedy. It could be that a few words you used are amplified in the person's mind, taken out of context or overblown after the fact. If the person shares their distorted perspective with others, the others may pick up the offense and blame you for the negative result. Thus you must be careful to use words which are received with the same meaning you intended. If you miss the mark you need to own up to it as soon as you become aware. Do what you can to keep this stimulation as an ongoing conversation, not an event. It may take some time for the love and good deeds to start to emerge.

Describing the failure of someone behind their back won't help them. Get out in front and consider your words and tactics in advance. But be sure to build your skill at stimulating others to love and good deeds. Your church needs it and our world will suffer without your help.

Your Take

1. Who immediately comes to your mind that could use a good nudge? What is your plan to nudge them forward in the right way? Who can help you develop that plan?
2. The great need in every church is for leaders to set the example. What leaders in your church are letting you down? When are you going to have a private conversation designed to move them forward?
3. When you attempt to get more out of others is it working for you? Or do you need to learn better techniques to get the results you are looking for?

~ 18 ~

Say Again

"I myself am convinced, my brothers and sisters, that you yourselves are full of goodness, filled with knowledge and competent to instruct one another." (Romans 15:14, also Colossians 3:16)

The more you know about any field of learning and endeavor the more you realize that you don't know it all. It is as if all the learning about the subject is contained in a large library and all you have knowledge of is in one skinny book on one shelf. Because there is always more to know you might think you know too little. Then someone who knows less than you comes along and is in awe of all you know. Realize that you don't have to know everything to become the teacher of someone else. You just have to know more than they know.

Wendy's Take

Growing up one of our sons loved his skateboard. Then when we went on vacation to a Christian resort he saw something else that took his fancy. The owner possessed a unicycle and taught Rob how to ride it. Every summer he spent hours honing his skill (not the easiest!) which became more developed when he somehow obtained his own. Someone asked recently how one dismounts a unicycle – the answer being push forward and fall off. When in Grade five his daughter decided she wanted to learn to ride that old unicycle and now she has become quite an expert. Her twin sister is following suit and so the tradition has been passed along because of good instruction. They both have purchased their own unicycles with a little help from their parents. Hopefully they will not follow the example of Rob's friend who rides a ten foot high unicycle. That's a long way down to fall!

The New Testament is full of examples of excellent teaching for making strong disciples of Jesus – from Jesus himself to John to Paul to numerous others. As a result the Gospel message has been passed along through the ages. A committed capable follower of Christ should be given opportunities and stretched beyond their comfort zone so that much more can be accomplished in themselves and their eventual chosen ministry of service. Much vision and patience are required by church leadership for this to happen.

Gary's Take

Paul says this, *"I myself am convinced, my brothers and sisters, that you yourselves are full of goodness, filled with knowledge and competent to instruct one another."* (Romans 15:14) But Paul had never been to Rome so how could he know?

We don't know how the church in Rome started. The Bible doesn't tell us. Other historical sources tell us there were Jews in Rome who had an uneasy relationship with the governing powers. Perhaps some from the Day of Pentecost mentioned in Acts 2 went home and spread the Gospel. Rome was a long way from Jerusalem and somehow the Gospel got there.

Two important leaders in the New Testament were Aquila and Priscilla. Paul met them in Corinth after the Jews were expelled from Rome. He spent a lot of time with them working in the tent making business. (Acts 18:1-4) Probably Paul learned all or most of what he knew about the church in Rome from his discussions with them. At the end of his letter to the Romans Paul mentions a long list of names of friends and acquaintances. Perhaps Aquila and/or Priscilla told Paul about their old friends from Rome. Some think Peter was the key person starting the church in Rome but there is no evidence from the Bible about that.

Let's work with the assumption that Aquila and Priscilla became Jewish believers while they were in Rome. We don't know that from the Bible. We do know that Paul went to see them as his first contact when he got to Corinth. It might have been the tentmaking network that linked them or the church or both. In any case, we know that these two people with a tent making business left with Paul after "*some time*"(Acts 18:18) and Paul dropped them off in Ephesus. In Ephesus Aquila and Priscilla met another man, Apollos and tuned him up on his knowledge. (Acts 18:24-25) Then somehow by the time Paul wrote the church in Rome, Aquila and Priscilla were back there because Paul asked the church to greet them and their house church. (Romans 16:3-4)

Paul's confidence in all the believers in Rome seems to have something to do with these key disciples. Now remember, they are not vocational missionaries; they run a tent-making business. I am guessing they had franchises of this business in Rome, Corinth and Ephesus. Wherever they were they created heavy involvement in the church and in teaching in it.

Now back to that anchor verse. Paul says that all the brothers and sisters were "*competent to instruct one another.*" (Romans 15:14) He doesn't presume they needed any special professional to do the teaching. They all had elements of the truth of the Gospel to share with each other. Maybe Aquila and Priscilla got things started but they went away to Corinth first and then Ephesus before they got back to Rome. Many others were raised up to carry the teaching load.

That is how it is supposed to work. Some churches just go into a holding pattern if their pastor moves on to another post. Not good. A strong church has many teachers, not just one. Most of those are people with jobs and other responsibilities to carry. That was true in Rome and it should be true where you live. Perhaps the Lord has bigger things for you in a teaching ministry because you too are competent to instruct.

As with each concept in this book there is a "*one another*" component here. Every Christian has power for this. That is the root meaning of the word translated "*competent.*" Power for what? Power to admonish, warn, counsel and exhort – the root meaning of the word for "*instruct*" used here.

This might come as a surprise to you but you are designated by the Lord himself as a powerful source to stimulate others to right living. The newest believer can point out what they notice to someone who seems bored by their Christian and church life. It isn't just for those with the special ability to teach.

When someone loses their way, often someone says, "I wondered what was going on there." But by then it is too late. The time to use instructing power is in the early moments – not when it may be too late. Speak up.

Do so with grace and in private but speak up. The person you are admonishing might not take it well at the time and tell you it is none of your business. But it is your business. Paul said so. However, the people to whom he said it originally were the ones "*full of goodness*" and "*filled with knowledge.*" So make sure you yourself are headed in the right direction and then speak up. You may find decades later that the one you instructed and who initially rejected your powerful encouragement comes back to say thank you. You might change the course of a life even though you don't realize it at the time.

This is only one component of our mutual responsibility so don't go overboard. It is very unattractive to have someone running around looking for people to criticize. This isn't about pointing out the wrongs; it is all about helping people find their way to a better life. All the "*one anothers*" hang together as a unit with the center point of "*love one another.*"

Your Take

1. Who in your church instructs you on a personal basis?
2. Who do you instruct on a personal basis?
3. Who is being left out on having someone to instruct them personally? What should you do about that?

~ 19 ~

I Attend Building U

"Build each other up."
(1 Thessalonians 5:11)

Building is a process. It takes a while and it isn't obvious from the start what the finished project will look like. That is, it isn't obvious if you can't see in your head what the plans on paper are saying. Randomly built places look like, well, randomly built places. Development of all kinds has to start somewhere – like in a Building University. Personal development starts where you are. With a good plan the end product is quite useful and sometimes impressive.

Wendy's Take

I was very impressed one day when participating in our church seniors' knitting and crocheting class. Rose unexpectedly attended for the first time. She lives with her daughter and family. Her homeland is Granada. Since she doesn't drive she took the bus to get to the church.

Rose had some experience early on in her life with crocheting but really wanted to learn to knit. One expert knitter in the group immediately helped her choose some wool and needles. She cast on a row of stitches to get her started making a scarf but then had to leave to take her husband to a doctor's appointment. Another experienced knitter thoughtfully took over teaching. Val's instructions were very simple, easily breaking down the task at hand step by step. She was so patient with Rose as she repeated her instructions over and over again. She encouraged her to keep going even though she was making some mistakes and the tension of her stitches was quite tight. Every once in a while, Val would commend her by saying, "That's excellent!"

By the time I had to leave too, Rose was well on her way to mastering a new craft with her new found friends. Her confidence was being built up. I watched these two ladies continuing to work for a few minutes more and then I went away rejoicing over what had just occurred. I know that this free gift of love for the homeless will be eventually received. I presume that person will be gratefully impressed as well.

Gary's Take

In the West, we live in a fiercely independent world. People who want to live one way are frustrated when someone tells them they must live another way. Rules that seem reasonable applied to everyone else don't seem reasonable when applied to oneself. But without rules there is chaos. When there is a green traffic signal there is a corresponding red light because people are going the other way too. The person who waits for all the lights to turn green will never get out of their driveway. We all have to agree on the meaning of green and red lights or our independence will get us nowhere.

When Paul uses the term *"build"* he is using a term that means house building in its raw sense but is applied to human building. How is humanity built up? There must be an accumulation of knowledge over time. That knowledge must be passed on. When it became easier to codify knowledge and pass it on through the mass production of books, knowledge exploded. Thanks Mr. Gutenberg! The printing press was a great idea.

In one decade we saw the explosion of availability of knowledge in the development of the Internet. Then the telephone became a global encyclopedia in your pocket. But it was too hard to enter letters one at a time so they made it easier by having you just hold the phone near your mouth and ask it as if it was human. Now you can ask the device across the room your question. If it doesn't know the answer today, when enough people ask the same question the answer is developed. This is getting easier.

So ask your device, "What is one Christian's responsibility to another?" Or more specifically, "How is a Christian supposed to build another Christian up?" C'mon now, there are supposed to be a couple of billion of us on this planet. Surely someone has worked out a good answer. Actually, if you do try that you will get hundreds of thousands of potential answers. Many of them are worth trying.

We don't suffer from a lack of ideas. We do suffer from enough Christians accepting their job as the one to build up another. And when one does invest in building up a person, that person is responsible to re-invest back in others. This process of the Christian development of the person is not just an individual pursuit; it is a *"one another"* dynamic trust.

Every Christ-follower is given this powerful stewardship to roll up their sleeves and get their hands dirty working on the construction project that is at least one other person at a time. Don't hide behind the weak excuse that you have enough to work on in your own life. Don't think that your primary responsibility with the members of your own household is the outer limits of your stewardship. Your family is only the beginning.

Building is action. The best buildings start with a plan. The plan may need some tearing down first but the focus is always on the building up. When a person has a picture of what they can become they are more likely to let you work with them on that construction.

The first thing many (probably most) Christians need is someone to help them see the plan for their life and believe it can become real over time. The best healers are the ones who themselves were once weak and have become stronger. They were once themselves wounded and still bear the scars. Sometimes those scars are on the inside and never need to become public. The internal memory may be enough of a reminder about the help another needs. At other times, the scars and memories are easily seen in the public history or even in bodily scars.

Positive building only happens in each life as we individually realize the need for it and accept personal responsibility. While the mess we find ourselves in may not be all of our own making, it is our personal responsibility to see to it that we get out of the mess. That being said, it is very, very difficult to get out of big messes without a helping hand or two. I firmly believe that you need at least one person as your mentor. And everyone you know needs a mentor as well. You have the incredible opportunity to be the mentor for someone who walks behind you. You can be the life builder for that one person. Nobody can help everybody but every Christian can help somebody.

If you feel like you have nobody to look to, you are not alone. That is a common complaint. Responsibility. Find someone. And in the interim find a good example from history to look to. If there is nobody in front of you it is lonely and difficult but you still must help those following behind. And of course, in the ultimate sense you have Jesus to follow. Study him; don't invent a Jesus in your own image and bring Him down to your level. Read and re-read the Gospels and then follow Him.

Think of the church as a great collective building project where everyone is swarming together to joyfully get the job done. One teaching another. Another encouraging one. Side by side any building project is easier. That is true whether it be physical construction or the building up of the body of Christ.

Your Take

1. Honestly now, have you accepted your responsibility to build up the others in your church? What evidence would you supply to prove that?
2. What regular actions do you take to build up others in the body?
3. If you are currently "under employed" in the building business, what informal role can you assign yourself to build up the others around you in your church? How will you learn to develop in that role?

~ 20 ~

Let Me Help You

"Carry each other's burdens, and in this way you will fulfill the law of Christ."
(Galatians 6:2)

A general rule held by people in western civilization is that if you get all the pieces in the right place you can have a prosperous and a reasonably peaceful life. Then something goes wrong. Always.

It might look like you are climbing the right ladder for a while but inevitably you will hit some rotten rungs that break under your feet. In the end everyone carries a heavy load. They may disguise the load from public observation but you will never go far wrong when you assume that under the tarp is a heavy load. The discussion is not about the load as much as it is about how you are going to carry it.

Wendy's Take

One of my many roles in life is grocery shopper. Each week I head over to our local grocery store where sometimes I wonder if I really am in Canada for all the different languages being spoken. It has become our mission field with the arrival of newcomers from everywhere. I select the items that I want, put them in the cart, pay for them and bag them. If I can manage to get them in the car – a task that is getting more difficult the older I get – then Gary will carry them into our house upon my return. We make a good team that way.

Another role that I own is church goer. Most believe that they are to attend church weekly to worship God which is a true and vital concept. But it is just as important to go to church to meet up with and talk to the like-minded people there. Paul exhorts us, *"Carry each other's burdens, and in this way you will fulfill the law of Christ."* (Galatians 6:2)

If we don't spend more time with fellow Christians how else will we get to know them better? How else will we be able to learn in a more in-depth way about their struggles so that we can carry their burdens home with us? Superficial chatter doesn't really get anyone anywhere, wouldn't you agree? During the rest of the week as the Holy Spirit prods our thinking we can mull over what was conveyed, specifically pray for the need and possibly help them find a solution in dealing with the ongoing pain. That also is wonderful teamwork.

Gary's Take

Burdens can go unnoticed if we are not careful. There are a series of small irritations that intercept our path. Getting out of the rain in a thunderstorm is uncomfortable but getting out of the way of a hurricane isn't so easy. A hurricane is no small inconvenience. When one hits, people tend to work together in the clean up. But at other times we won't be so thoughtful in supplying the help people need unless we are careful to notice.

If we are not careful we will let our own small inconveniences seem like real burdens. When we invest too much in working around our own little irritants and chores we have little mental stamina left to notice the bigger burdens others are carrying.

"*Religion that God our Father accepts as pure and faultless is this: to look after orphans and widows in their distress and to keep oneself from being polluted by the world.*" (James 1:27) That is a verse packed in among various direct instructions about our behavior. It would appear that noticing and responding to the needs of two groups in particular might have been missing in the early church. Widows and orphans are isolated single people who don't have as much, if any, family support. They have special day-to-day burdens. This isn't about organizing a church ministry to widows or orphans, as good an idea as that may be. It is about the personal responsibility of every Christian to do something about needy groups like that. This verse isn't specifically a "*one another*" verse. It seems to highlight any and all widows and orphans. However, in Galatians 6:10 Paul suggests prioritizing the people who are believers. "*Therefore, as we have opportunity, let us do good to all people, especially to those who belong to the family of believers.*"

Wendy mentioned grocery shopping. Usually I stay home because that is her preference. She would rather think without me hovering. So far she has been able to handle getting things from the cart to the car. But once she is back home the shorter trip from the car to the kitchen is a little bigger. But we work it out easily. What about the widows and widowers? What about the single parents? They often don't have anyone to support them in such tasks. Does anyone notice?

Here is the thing. If you don't help others with smaller items like carrying groceries, how will you ever expect anyone to share with you the heavier hidden burdens they are carrying? When you show support in smaller things others may trust you with bigger loads.

You are more aware of your own bigger loads that you carry alone than you are of the loads others carry. There are times when you yearn for some help and understanding. Bear in mind that others feel the longing for someone to help them carry a burden or two as well.

Do you recall at the beginning of this book we noted that in this "*one anothering*" business we are likely to think we do more for others than they do for us? That could be true. So what? We all need to understand that we know something about our own struggles but we don't automatically know the other person's heavy load. Many people keep their struggles to themselves. That can be good and it can be bad. On the one hand, *"for each one should carry their own load"* (Galatians 6:5) points to personal responsibility. On the other hand, we can't *"carry each other's burdens"* (Galatians 6:2) if we don't figure out what burdens exist to carry for others.

Others aren't going to ask for help until they are desperate. Jump in and offer before desperation sets in. Even if their fierce independence kicks in and they refuse your help they will appreciate the offer.

It is your activity of investing time in carrying the burdens of others that brings a special kind of fulfillment. You get to *"fulfill the law of Christ."* (Galatians 6:2) While Paul doesn't explain what that is, I am confident it is the new command to *"love one another."* (John 13:34) That is easier in theory than in practice because it means we will have to set aside what we would rather do – or even need to do – to take the time necessary to help someone else.

Your Take

1. Who in your church orbit has a burden to carry that you have helped with? What difference did that help make to your relationship?
2. How does it make you feel when someone helps you without expecting anything in return? How do you make yourself aware you can give others similar positive and comforting experiences?
3. When some burden-carrying need crosses your path this week, will you drop what you are doing and go and help? How will you find the time to fit in the activity that was displaced? Or do you even need to?

~ 21 ~

I'll Take Care of That

"Serve one another humbly in love."
(Galatians 5:13)

Service without compensation is in short supply. Western society has evolved into a "pay for play" world. Fewer people do their own house repairs and fewer yet give time to help another. There is a better way.

Wendy's Take

Susan was a struggling single mom raising her teenaged son and daughter. She had become a member at the new church plant in town that Gary and I helped start. Gary was the founding pastor. It was decided by the board that this lady needed help to encourage her day-to-day living. Her husband had left her with unfinished house renovations. She had no kitchen sink. She could only draw water for cooking from her bathroom tub. We managed to steal her away from her home one weekend on a baby-sitting assignment for a family in the church. We even let the air out of her tires so that she couldn't drive her car home for whatever reason.

Early Friday evening a small crew arrived on the scene to get a head start on the work. Up to 30 more friends came by Saturday to continue the demolition and reconstruction. We were able to cut the lawn, tidy the garden, lay new carpet, install a kitchen sink, paint walls throughout, plus whatever else we discovered that needed repair along the way. Her neighbors were very curious about what we were doing. Even one couple came to church later on and accepted the Lord because they saw this love in action. Other passersby thought it was a garage sale with all the garbage thrown on the front lawn. When Susan returned home much later that day she was extremely overwhelmed by what had been accomplished and the love that was shown her by a church family that served her that weekend. We were as good as any makeover television program today!

Gary's Take

The concept of serving others without pay for the activity seems foreign to many. Even in homes children are bribed to do what they ought to do just because they are in the family. Of course, that is not true in every case. But it is more and more true that parents live by an "if/then" relationship with their children. "If you clean your room then I will let you play your video game." Then the negotiations take a turn, "If I clean my room for four weeks in a row without you asking will you buy me the new video game everyone else has?" The stakes just got higher and the child was diminished. Doing one's chores is what one does just because.

Service in and through the church has taken a big hit. Tasks that used to be completed by volunteers are farmed out to more and more paid staff. Careful. There might just be a correlation between the loss of relationships and personal development because of the trend. People build relationships with others because they spend time together. The relationship build is much stronger when it is reinforced by completing tasks together. The engagement of working on difficult tasks together has amazing results. Pounding a nail beside someone with a saw is a bonding experience. An older person teaching another younger person a skill is unforgettable by both. When that skill is applied to supplying help for someone in need the results are even more solid. There are many places to serve in every community and when that service radiates from a local church the church prospers. One can serve at a community food bank and that is good. But it is even more powerful if people in any one church band together to perform such a service.

The standard excuse is, "I'm too busy to help with that." And since the person fills in 24 hours every day that is true. With their priorities set as they are, they are too busy for anything else. This is not about not having enough time. We all get the same allotment of time. It is about setting aside something in favor of something else. Less sports; more service. Fewer movies; more service. Put down the games and use the phone to find out what more you can do to help someone in need with humility. This is about what you choose to do much more than what the church chooses to organize.

Paul gave clear instruction to slaves that ought to apply across the board, *"Whatever you do, work at it with all your heart, as working for the Lord, not for human masters, since you know that you will receive an inheritance from the Lord as a reward. It is the Lord Christ you are serving."* (Colossians 2:23-24) When a believer grasps the concept it is a game changer. Acts of service where Christians lean into the opportunity are a wonderful way to demonstrate love for Jesus. It takes the heat off. It no longer matters that you are alone in your service where others ought to be helping. That is their loss. Their loss should sadden you deeply but never make you feel cheated. You get to dig down deep and work an hour longer walking a mile farther for the Lord. What a blast of blessing!

Service is personal even when it is given to a whole group. When you serve you get to know people better and they you. You get to pick up some tips about how to do it from those working around you. You hear the stories of life in the midst of repetitive work. You bond with others. On and on! But that is not the whole story. It gets better. Paul tells those slaves who have no rights of ownership that their reward is an inheritance stored up for them on the other side of the great divide. That injects hope and joy on this side.

What sorts of service are there? The list is endless. If you have knowledge about a topic you can share it with those who are learning. You might not realize it but the farther down the road of life you walk and endure more potholes the more you have to share with others about how to keep from stumbling. You learn the shortcuts that seem unnecessary until you learn the hard way. You get to pass on simple rules like the carpenter who reminds the apprentice, "Measure twice; cut once." On the other side of such a relationship, if you don't know so much, you get to learn quickly and take away some of the tedious work like moving stuff.

Grunt work is good work. Notice the instruction about service includes the word "*humbly.*" Humble work requires humble service. There is a prime opportunity to show love. Look for the work nobody else wants because of its humble nature and start there. Perhaps an individual needs your service but would never ask because of the unpleasant nature of the work. Look for the work and gladly offer to do it. That is how you build a great inheritance.

Your Take

1. What service has been expected of you that you have thought unfair because others should also participate? How has your attitude robbed you of joy in serving Jesus?
2. Who in your orbit could use a little help from a friend? When are you going to fit that in?
3. What differences can you imagine in your church when you get together to take on a big service task like the story about Susan?

Give It!

This category of "*one anothers*" has the general characteristic that to fulfill them you have to displace your first instincts. The universe doesn't have you as a center despite how you started out. One of your first words was "mine."

Now it's time for you to see what you can give away to others.

~ 22 ~

I Hear Harmony

"Live in harmony with one another. Do not be proud, but be willing to associate with people of low position. Do not be conceited."
(Romans 12:16)

Harmonious living is an ideal seldom seen on a grand scale. The country to country harmony is shattered in many places. Even within any one country one group fails to live in harmony with another. Home living is in tatters in a high percentage of homes. A couple that once said, "I do" now says "I won't". Your church is here to make a difference in your community and set an example by the people of your church each learning how to live better and harmoniously.

Wendy's Take

"People can fight like cats and dogs!" I'm confident you have heard that saying before. Charlie came to live with us for a couple of months before our pastor and his family moved into their new home in Milton, Ontario. Their long-haired, feline monster is more dog-like as he followed us every where yapping for food or for affection. He was enjoying his life until our son's dog, Maverick showed up for a visit one weekend – a canine that is exuberantly friendly. Needless to say, there was lots of hissing and barking back and forth between these two. At one point as I sat in our living-room, all of a sudden I spotted a beige furry head hanging down from the shelf beside the staircase to the upstairs where he had taken refuge. Charlie was spying on his new acquaintance, being close but not too close. We lived with an upstairs cat and a downstairs dog for a couple of days. No harmony there.

You might not say that church folk can fight like cats and dogs but there definitely are tensions in a church when people don't get along for various reasons. Some look the other way so they can avoid greeting another with love if they are not on speaking terms. It doesn't take much for a small disagreement to fester for many a year. In one of our church building projects a gentleman even left the church because he didn't like the choice of color for the outside brick. Others religiously keep tabs on what someone else may or may not be contributing to the church life. Harmony requires undaunted work to build a positive atmosphere. All must realize that selfishness and self-centeredness are not a part of the equation.

Gary's Take

Many Bible translations use the word *"harmony"* to translate the concept in the first phrase of Romans 16:12. Literally the raw meaning at the heart of the matter is a word rendered in different ways. It means "think, judge, direct the mind to, seek for, observe, care for." We might say, "Get your head in the game!" The word along side it that creates the legitimate translation as *"harmony"* is the word normally translated, "he, she, it, they, them, same." Not one concept against another but a singular concept. So we might say, "Get with the program!"

It would be easy to do that if there was always one known plan. Harmony is easy when everyone adopts "my" ideas for a plan. But what happens when there are – as there always are – multiple ideas about how things should be?

Sometimes there are alternate plans that have equal merit. As the saying goes, "There is more than one way to skin a cat." (Who ever skins that cat anyway?) It is always true that a good plan for today is better than a perfect plan for tomorrow. Today is all we have. Harmony requires engagement in an agreed plan for today. Many conflicts happen in a church when people have different plans and are not aware of, or don't agree with, the one plan that is supposed to be implemented.

In order to create harmony everyone has to come at the collective experience with a readiness to let go of their own pet ideas. Thus Paul follows, *"Live in harmony with one another"* with "*Do not be proud.*" (Romans 12:6)

Same word, "think" and in this case literally "high thinking." Let me try and put that together, "Think as one; don't think your idea is the best one just because it is your idea." Oh, and just in case you missed the rest of the verse, "Be open to the ideas of the person who is lower than you in the org chart. You are not as hot as you may think." The four ideas in this one verse hang together as one. Harmony requires all four parts. Look at the verse carefully for yourself. Check it out in other translations. Here is one you are less likely to find: Aramaic Bible in Plain English, "*And whatever you esteem about yourselves do also about your brethren. Do not esteem high opinions, but go out to those who are humble, and do not be wise in your opinions of yourselves.*" (Romans 12:6)

Leaders are called to lead in the developing of this harmony. Clearly from this verse we can see that harmony is not something imposed from the top. The lowly person's perspective must be given serious consideration. Churches thrive when all the people believe their perspective matters and is carefully considered. Churches suffer when the people judge that the leaders have big egos. It is not for leaders to hold "town hall meetings" pretending they are listening and then just go on their merry way without adjusting the plan based on the input. Sometimes a simple change in schedule brings relaxation to the group. Sometimes it takes a small adjustment in job descriptions. Acts 6:1-7 gives a wonderful example about how they created harmony in the early church. That is a pattern to follow. They had a problem and found a solution that pleased the whole group because they listened.

Here is a quick overview.

1. **The Context:** The presenting problem had to do with the social welfare system implemented by this new church. They distributed food every day for needy widows. (Acts 6:1)
2. **The Complaint:** There were two different kinds of Jewish widows in this emerging church. The distribution wasn't equitable and so there was a lack of harmony. (Acts 6:1)
3. **The Control:** The Apostles called the disciples together to find the solution to the problem. They came to the meeting with a solution in mind. (Acts 6:2)
4. **The Clarification:** They recommended that the church choose seven men who could concentrate on the food distribution. (Acts 6:3-4)
5. **The Consideration:** The Twelve left it up to the people. (Acts 6:5)
6. **The Consensus:** The proposal pleased the whole group. (Acts 6:5)

7. **The Commissioning:** We could imagine the seven were presented to The Twelve with confidence and pride. The Apostles accepted the choice and ordained them to the task with a ceremony of prayer and laying on of hands. (Acts 6:6)

This story is a descriptive one and not designed to provide a set of rules on how to operate. However, it gives us a wonderful template to consider as we develop a philosophy of church decision making that involves everyone and creates harmony.

Your Take

1. Who consistently throws sand in the gears at your church? What can you do to ease that person into a more harmonious approach?
2. What facts are some people failing to consider as your church develops a harmonious ministry plan? Can you find another way to express those facts to move things forward? Are there illustrations or success stories that will win people to one mind?
3. What is your personal role in bringing your church into greater harmony? Are there some people you need to spend time with and listen to their perspective so you can adjust your own mind?

~ 23 ~

You're Good

"Do nothing out of selfish ambition or vain conceit. Rather, in humility value others above yourselves" (Philippians 2:3)

Assertiveness is highly valued in our world. The problem comes when an individual seems to be able only to speak up for their own so-called rights. Paul is teaching something very different.

Wendy's Take

We have an insightful pastor friend in his later 80s who connects with Gary a few times each week on the phone or email or even video chat. He loves to tell stories about what he has experienced in his life through the years. The latest one is about his wife. They both live in a retirement residence not too far from us. He lives in an apartment on his own and she in the nursing complex nearby. She has suffered with dementia for about the past eight years. It must be very hard on him as he watches her day by day and finds himself patiently answering the same questions over and over again.

Someone asked him if he was still preaching these days. He quickly retorted, "I preach every day, Sunday to Saturday, fours hours each day!" He was referring to all the time he spends with his dear wife caring for her. Upon occasion he will take her for a drive and will drop by our house for a brief visit in the driveway. (He phones us to say he is waiting for someone to come out). He asked her not too long ago if she liked all the kisses that he gives her daily. She responded immediately, "Yes! It makes me feel worthwhile." What a clear statement from someone who struggles with her mind most of the time. She knows she is loved.

Billy Graham noted a few years ago that he had prepared himself all along on how to die but not on growing old. Our friend with his unique sense of humor is teaching us a wonderful lesson on how to grow old while continuing to value his beloved companion no matter the stage of life he finds her to be in.

Gary's Take

You are the only one who can express exactly what you want or believe you need. Nobody can read your mind. Even when someone knows you well they can only guess at what you are thinking. Your perspective matters but it may not be the only viewpoint. A group suffers when the one with the most persuasive manner and voice dominates a decision.

This key verse is absolute. There is no room whatsoever for you to make a choice or a suggestion out of your own selfish ambition or empty pride. However, it is easy to be blind to your own emptiness if you are not careful. Jealousy is an emotion we feel intensely. We are all well-tuned to notice when something doesn't seem right in our own eyes. Therefore, you might not recognize that the suggestion you are advocating is based solely on self-interest and you are only being jealous by advocating for your own interest all the while claiming your viewpoint is better for all. Paul says, *"Do nothing"* (Philippians 2:3) out of your own empty desires.

If you are a church leader you must watch yourself. A preacher finds it easy to speak against his own pet peeves. If he was raised in a certain way he will be well aware of the failings in his past and want to assure such failings are eliminated in his present. But it could be that others didn't have the same experience and therefore don't feel the same way. Rebelling against an inferior past will only lead to different deficiencies in the present. For example, if you think the church of yesterday had rules that were too strict you will likely advocate a set of lax rules or a set of rules that are just as narrow in a different way. Here is a specific example. If in your youth you were forced to dress in a certain way you will be susceptible to attempting to create a similar culture forcing people but with a different dress code you think is more apropos today. Different dress; same rigidity.

You might have a personal preference for a certain kind of music in your church that isn't the same as others. If a particular piece of music moves people in the right direction, then even if you don't like it there is no reason to ban it from use in your church. That is simply "*vain conceit.*" It could go so far as you insisting that particular music is evil. That is hard to argue from the Bible. To repeat, if it moves people in the right direction, where is the sin?

Selfish agendas squelch productivity and progress. You don't need to win every time. In fact, you don't need to win any time as long as everyone is valued, their individual needs carefully taken into account and the framework you all agree upon is the whole counsel of God.

You don't need to cover the themes that are of interest to you but not to the others. What you find fascinating may not be so compelling as you think.

Humility is the characteristic to cultivate much more than assertiveness. You don't need to stand up for yourself anywhere near as much as you need to stand up for each other.

You might have been looking for the words "one another" in the translation above. It is hard to translate smoothly into English but here it is in a more literal translation (Berean Literal Bible). "*... nothing according to self-interest or according to vain conceit, but in humility be esteeming one another surpassing themselves.*"

The best way to uncover the needs of others is to ask and then listen to the answer. Sometimes you may need to listen more deeply than the other person is speaking. They may be stating a felt need that rests on a misplaced value. Behavior is based on thoughts, feelings and attitudes which grow over time based on our upbringing and culture. The influence of family, peers and mentors shape us. This is what the Bible calls a *"worldly point of view"* (2 Corinthians 5:16) all around us and sadly, in us. Therefore we all must constantly breath out the toxicity of sin and breath in the fresh power of the Spirit. That's why John said, "*If we confess our sins, he is faithful and just and will forgive us our sins and purify us from all unrighteousness.*" (1 John 1:9)

So in this world where we are all infected with debilitating viruses of sin how can we ever get a good perspective? Paul's answer is to compensate for our self-centeredness by deliberately placing more value on the other person than we do on ourselves.

Your Take

1. How often do you find yourself asking, "Am I missing something I should be taking into account?" How do you know that is often enough to show you value others above yourself?
2. What evidence can you point to that would suggest others know you care more about them than about yourself?
3. What processes do you have in place to keep yourself from acting out of selfish ambition or conceit?

~ 24 ~

I Accept You

"Accept one another, then, just as Christ accepted you, in order to bring praise to God."
(Romans 15:7)

Everyone hungers for acceptance. It is not always clear what that means. On the surface it might appear that the person wants to be accepted for their lifestyle choices. But it goes much deeper. It isn't about looks, manner, style or choices. It is about something much deeper in the soul beyond all the scars.

Wendy's Take

Harry was a unique individual whom we met through a church where Gary was serving as an interim pastor. He would regularly attend their food bank lunches on Fridays at noon. Gary was always intrigued by this elderly man as he seemed to be different than others attending. Gary knew he had a background story to tell. One day a volunteer asked him if he wanted some food to take home to his son. He retorted, "How do you know about my son?" She replied, "You told us about him before." He quickly responded, "Why do you people care so much?" This was just one example of how these faithful volunteers accepted anyone no matter how gruff and despairing they happened to be. It was and continues to be very impressive.

Gary also accepted Harry for where he was at in life. Their friendship grew through Gary inviting him out for coffee or to a couple of Christian movies. His story soon came out that he had been a prosperous funeral director in town for many a year; but unfortunately had gotten involved with "pharmaceutical" dealers. One of his dealers squealed on him and he found himself in jail. Upon returning to society he had to cope with the loss of his marriage, business and most importantly his dignity.

Just before we moved away, Gary had another coffee chat with him and carefully explained the Gospel message again. We learned later that his health quickly deteriorated thereafter. Just before he died a gentleman from the church led him to the Lord who freely accepted him into his heavenly family as one of his precious sons no matter what he had been caught up with in his earthly life. You never know!

Gary's Take

The song says this, "Jesus loves me. This I know for the Bible tells me so." Actually, the Bible doesn't say your name and connect it to the love of Jesus. But the love of God in Christ reaches to you as an individual within the scope of the *"whoever"* of the famous verse John 3:16. So the song got it right. It started as a poem in a novel spoken to comfort a dying child. The tune and chorus were added later. Since 1862 that song has captured the hearts of countless millions.

Why? Acceptance. Jesus accepts me so much that I can be sure he loves me.

I'm just like you – not what I wish I was. One day I will be perfect. How do I know? The Bible tells me so. I am in a fabulous group according to Hebrews 11. And in that group the promise is, *"God had planned something better for us so that only together with us would they be made perfect."* (Hebrews 11:40)

If you have truly trusted in Christ alone for your salvation and have put your life in his hands for direction on earth and on into eternity, you too will be perfect when he comes or when he takes you to your new home. That gives me chills every time I contemplate it! You and me – perfect! Whooo hooo!

Now, I know there are people in or around the edges of your life you are not sure about. You wonder how they could ever live as they do and still be in the company of the redeemed. You may wonder about some famous person who says the right words but lives a hypocritical life. You don't have to answer for them, just for yourself. Learn from their weakness by applying the standard of examination to yourself that you wish they applied to themselves.

You might not find some people as attractive as others. There are some people who get on your nerves or get you down. It could be profitable for you to get to know those people better. You might like them a little more if you got to know them a little more.

Accepting one another doesn't mean that we agree with or like everything about the other person. It does mean that we strive to apply the same standard that Christ applied.

The further people wander from God, the more they wander from the order created by God. When a society fails to have cultural norms based on God's revelation, there is no end of evil and discord. Polygamy, sexual deviations, cannibalism and demon worship pile on to the more expected human sins such as greed, lust, pride and envy. We never have to accept the validity of any of these no matter how far the society wanders from God. We can expect society to normalize convenient sins just as child sexual abuse was normalized in ancient Rome. That is, we can expect that if we are not the salt and light Jesus commanded us to be. The world has to see the city on the hill we create that cannot be hidden. (Matthew 5:13-16) The worse things get the more we must love people toward the kingdom while not condoning their aberrant lives. When they find the Savior those old vices will slip away over time if we live out all the "*one anothers.*"

The more progress you see in your own life, the more capacity you ought to have to accept those who live and think as you once did. You will find much more acceptance for others if you review regularly how the Lord rescued you from a path you were on or a path you came close to taking. Every human is a few small steps away from a terrible slide into sin. Sin doesn't need to look disgusting to the world to be disgusting. For example, the greed and self-centeredness of some wealthy people is reprehensible regardless of the brand names on their clothes. It is way too easy to forget what you have been saved from. That is not a forgetting in terms of memory loss but a forgetting to take into account that you too could have ended up in a much bigger mess but for the grace of God.

You know the wretch you were or were on the edge of becoming. I once was lost but now am found; was blind but now I see. Someone should write a song about that!

Your Take

1. Do you have trouble accepting others? Why? No really, why?
2. Do you sit with and converse with the least accepted people in your church?
3. When was the last time you invited the least accepted people into your home to share a meal with some of the more prominent members? How did that go?

~ 25 ~

I Feel That

"Be kind and compassionate to one another, forgiving each other, just as in Christ God forgave you." (Ephesians 4:32)

Never before in history have people been so aware of what is going wrong on the globe. Local concerns were always known but the global impact of difficulties is overwhelming. Knowledge is not concern but it could lead there. We all have to pick our concerns carefully and then act on them.

Wendy's Take

Two months before Christmas countless churches encourage their attenders to take a shoebox home to fill with various items – dolls, cars, puzzles, socks, crayons, notebooks, bar soap, combs etc. – for a boy or a girl depending on the age. I have participated in this well organized program of giving a few times. It must be exciting for the workers to hand out these gifts to needy children and watch the joy on their faces as they open their very own box of goodies.

Our daughter, Sara, and granddaughter, Cassidy decided to go on a mission trip this past summer to Peru for ten days. One of their many tasks was to travel to a garbage site and hand out water bottles to those scrounging for anything worthwhile at the dump. This is the way of life for these down-trodden people who do not have much hope for a different future.

All of our four children have travelled to other countries on short term mission trips at some point in their lives. What life changing experiences and super encouragement to the missionaries who have orchestrated these visits! They learned first hand how to be kind and compassionate to any poor souls whom God directed across their paths. There are lots and lots of missionary organizations to become involved in a similar ministry with much more modern conveniences and up-to-date communication technology today than ever before. We have no excuse not to be examples for others to take on a similar challenge in our own church, local community or overseas to show these compelling fruits of the Spirit.

Gary's Take

Most people are inspired when they see compassion in action. They make movies and TV programs about these things. It seems people take vicarious joy from watching others show extraordinary kindness.

Sometimes the word for compassionate is translated tender-hearted. Actually, the word is a compound word made up of the word for "good" and the word for "visceral organs." Literally that would be "good-guts." This is about having gut-level empathy for one another. The other word linked to this one another phrase is "kind." It means "to furnish what is useful." This is an action word not primarily a feeling word. Putting the two concepts together we get "put your gut-level feelings into action." Don't just feel it; do something useful. Being kind and compassionate is not a passive activity. Get involved with one another and help at a practical level.

No Christian can do everything but every Christian can do something.

The television commercials used to ask for about $30 a month to sponsor a needy child. Have you noticed that many of these appeals are now down to as low as $10 a month? One of my younger friends has invested a huge amount of money, effort and time creating a charity that asks for $1 a month. The cruel reality of our world is that it takes over $1 in effort and advertising to raise the first dollar from a new donor. And then the continued donations never continue forever and seldom does that one new donor recruit others of their friends to join the cause. Everyone can afford a few dollars; most people don't bother to give anything.

A few decades ago, to understand the industry, I took a minimum wage position as a telemarketer to raise money for a worthy cause working in a war torn area. No matter how much I genuinely poured my soul into the headset talking to people over the wires the response was meager. I was a little better at it than the others in the booths beside me but not much. It was hard work. At the end of a long day I travelled an hour to get to the call center and called to the west cost until midnight local time – 9pm their time. I thought I might die of fatigue before hitting the button to ask the computer to dial the next number. But as soon as someone answered I would show the interest from deep in my heart. Most people either just hung up or somewhat politely told me they couldn't help at this time. Even though I talked to over 50 people an hour I left my three hour shift only having found a few donors. When you added together the five hours expended it was not worth it financially for me and I knew it was minimally worth it for the charity. But it was much better than doing nothing.

Since that time research shows that the typical person has doubled their time in front of a screen. Bear in mind there was no "social media" back in the day; the Internet was barely up and running. Our exposure to the needs around the world has more than doubled but not our donations.

When Paul talks to the Ephesian church and encourages them to be kind and compassionate to one another he was not talking about global reach – in other places he does – but not here. He is focused on what was happening in the church he got to know so well because he invested between two and three years leading them. In his farewell message to the Ephesian elders he says in Acts 20:27, *"I have not hesitated to proclaim to you the whole will of God."* In paying attention to the believers in Ephesus, Paul knew they needed to be reminded to *"be kind and compassionate to one another."* (Ephesians 4:32) That presumes it was an area they needed to brush up on in the church. How could they ever reach the world with compassion if they weren't experiencing it at home?

In our day this is a both/and situation. Every believer should express kindness and compassion in their own local situation and also participate around the world. In terms of giving, most churches invest much more heavily at home than they do at a distance. Most people in local churches invest less in any giving at all than they do buying coffee at the drive-thru. That is probably not you because you show your concern by reading this book. But for most, it seems that buying a morning perk-me-up supplants the real need for kindness and compassion. I think Paul might have something to say about that if he visited your church.

Your Take

1. What exactly do you do on a regular basis that exhibits kindness and compassion? Is it enough?
2. What cause could you encourage others to join you with in partnership? Word of mouth is much more powerful than word of mouse.
3. How do you personally set the example of kindness and compassion in what you do and how much you give?

~ 26 ~

You First

"Submit to one another out of reverence for Christ."* *(Ephesians 5:21)

Submission isn't a quality loved by all because it is misunderstood and in some cases manipulatively and abusively applied. We need to get a good handle on this.

Wendy's Take

Families love owning pets. Our family learned when purchasing a puppy to choose one that didn't mind lying back in someone's arms, having its belly rubbed without squirming which showed its submissiveness. Our granddaughter, Kaiya, spent a lot of time researching what would be a good breed of dog for her family. And yes, the border collie she chose would come at every beck and call and loved to be cuddled – so much so that when our daughter visited our home recently with Kayley, now 40 pounds, all of a sudden she pounced up into Sara's lap. Someone needs to teach her that she is no longer a lap dog or a scaredy-cat.

The idea of submitting wives (Ephesians 5:22) has left a bad taste in countless minds because they don't understand it. Nervous lap dogs or deflated door mats who give in to every whim or fancy their husband demands do not help anyone, least of all themselves. I prefer to think of it as scheduling one's life around with lots of communication from both. There always has to be a head of the home, the one who has the final say, but decisions are made in pleasing accord with one another. The Christian couple is headed in the same direction peacefully. Likewise, this speaks to church life. The wise pastor or other church leader doesn't insist on or govern fellow church members into submission to get their own way. Happy church families are filled with people who take the other's viewpoints into consideration.

Gary's Take

The New Testament mentions about 100 people by name in connection with all the churches. There are probably more people than that connected with your church. We don't know much about many of these people who are only referred to a few times. We are left to fill in the story from a few clues and our own imaginative deductions.

For instance, let's look at Stephanas for a moment. Stephanas and his household were baptized by Paul as the first converts in the province. Thus we can assume there was a Mrs. Stephanas and enough children to decide together to be the ones to take on this new faith in Christ standing against the pagan norms in their city of Corinth. (1 Corinthians 1:16, 16:15)

There aren't any titles supplied here but collectively they served in the church with devotion to the Lord's people. Perhaps they had the first church of Corinth meeting in their own home. We know from the fiasco Paul talks about in 1 Corinthians that people left their own homes to go to a central place where they served the Lord's supper. (1 Corinthians 11:17-22) The church gathered exhibited divisions among the people. We don't know how many were in the church but we do know there were several households – just like your church. So should we think of Stephanas as the pastor of the church? He isn't called that. His colleagues Fortunatus and Achaicus along with Stephanas are called co-workers. That is a term Paul uses elsewhere to describe colleagues in various places. (Romans 16:3, 16:9, 16:21, 1 Thessalonians 3:2, 2 Corinthians 8:23, Philippians 2:25, 4:3, Colossians 4:10-11, Philemon 1, 24) It is a favorite term of Paul to describe those who devote their lives to labouring in the Gospel work. The Greek word is "*sunergeő*" from which we get the English word "synergy."

We are told to submit to people like this who join in the work. That may or may not apply to people with officially appointed positions. Stephanas was the first convert in his province and naturally would have been given a position of honor as the church grew. Maybe they officially appointed him and maybe he just jumped in and started serving people. Maybe both. I suspect they named people to some official role of leadership after they proved their worth. They had earned their role as first among the equals. They had attained trust. We have a pattern today to bring in a new leader from somewhere else and give that person attributed trust based on their former experience elsewhere where they have proved themselves. The more natural evolution is to appoint leaders from within which seems to be the general pattern of the New Testament.

One more thing we know about Stephanas is that he along with Fortunatus and Achaicus traveled (probably across the sea to Ephesus) to meet Paul and give him a boost. *"I was glad when Stephanas, Fortunatus and Achaicus arrived, because they have supplied what was lacking from you. For they refreshed my spirit and yours also. Such men deserve recognition."* (1 Corinthians 16:17-18) Paul's commendation of them gives a glimpse into their character and into the support (financial?) that the church of Corinth supplied for the apostolic ministry.

In all this we get the clue of mutually submissive relationships among church leaders who were all on the same team. They were sensitive to each other and arranged their affairs for mutual benefit. Paul tells us to submit to such people. (1 Corinthians 16:16)

Then we leave Corinth and arrive at the Ephesian church where Paul gives direct instruction about submission with slaves to masters and wives to husbands. But the key point is, *"Submit to one another out of reverence for Christ."* (Ephesians 5:21)

In a well-ordered church there is a lot of submission going on. In fact, the idea of arranging our own lives as church participants under the others around us is a key characteristic. It would be hard to imagine scheduling conflicts in the New Testament church they couldn't work out because of the circumstance of one person pressing their personal calendar and imposing it on others. That ought to be true today as well.

A while back it was common to have "worship wars" over the style of music in church. What were we thinking? The older people are supposed to be the adults in the room. Submission in matters like these should be the character quality on all sides. The younger people will follow the Christlike example of those who have gone before when it is exhibited. The church in

Corinth had its problems but it appears that Stephanas and his family weren't part of that. May their tribe increase in your church!

Your Take

1. Would you say your church has harmony because people are willing to submit to one another? Where could you be a refresher like Stephanas?
2. As you look back, can you see instances where conflict arose in church? What can you learn from those difficult times?
3. In what ways do you experience the joy that comes from not having to have your own way?

~ 27 ~

It's Just You and Me

"Do not deprive each other except perhaps by mutual consent and for a time, so that you may devote yourselves to prayer. Then come together again so that Satan will not tempt you because of your lack of self-control. (1 Corinthians 7:5)

This is the only "*one another*" that applies to just two people. It might be easy to slip past it because of that fact – as many lists of *"one anothers"* do. But why should we do that when it is in the inspired list? How could we ignore it in a society obsessed with misdirected sex? That was a problem in the New Testament age too. Satan always wants to mess with God's good ideas so let's talk about it.

Wendy's Take

I have been dreading this one. As I have said earlier, I am a quiet person and I don't find it easy to talk about something as personal as sex. But here we go.

It breaks my heart when I see a marriage go awry. It happens far too often. Over the years we have been surprised by the real life stories of people we once had an active relationship with who walk away from each other. It is especially painful to see it in the church in which we are currently serving. I always wonder about what more we could have done to keep things from going into a ditch.

After a while you figure it out. It was about the sex in the marriage or lack thereof more often than not. Perhaps there were unrealistic expectations set by the consumption of material that created dissatisfaction. Perhaps one or other of the partners was simply not paying attention to the other's needs. Perhaps the busyness of life left one or the other or both partners too stressed out to pay attention. Perhaps it was one of the partners unwilling to express themselves properly to the other. I seldom know the facts. But I do know it is never right to deprive your partner of sex no matter what the pressures.

It may seem difficult to plan your sex life because you think you prefer spontaneity. But if it isn't happening spontaneously you have to find a way to build it in.

I won't go into any details about the differences between a man and a woman. I will leave that up to those who know more and are more comfortable talking about it. But I will say if you find that sex isn't as important to you as it once was, you had better figure out what is going wrong before it goes really wrong.

Gary's Take

This is a hard hitting verse if you let it hit hard. First of all, it must be said that this verse is about sexual relations between a married man and woman. There is no other legitimate expression of sex between (or perish the thought, among) humans. Sadly, some even experiment with animals. That makes me cringe but it has always been out there. God is the universe's primary fan of good sex between one man and one woman who are married to each other.

Understand why this is true. This isn't just about pleasure but it sure includes pleasure! It isn't just about procreation but with it of course there is procreation potential. Sex also includes the dynamic element of partnership. All three are important but I want to focus on the partnership part.

Speaking personally, Wendy and I married our best friend. Oh yes, we wanted the sex and we hoped for children but the thing that sealed the deal for us was that we liked each other as friends first. Perhaps that is why I want to talk about the partnership of a marriage.

Our marriage probably couldn't have lasted this long if the partnership didn't include the bonding sex created. The chemicals in our bodies create the bonding which comes only through sexual relations.

Our world – and worlds before us – have all the enticements to divorcing sexual expression from marriage. But that never ever has brought the human experience God designed us for. Many failed societies and societies headed for failure separated the commitment of marriage from sex. People commonly believe the lie that couples should see if they are "sexually compatible" before they marry. They fail to understand that so-called "sexual compatibility" can't possibly be properly developed outside of marriage. In the words from a very old song by The Carpenters, "Let's take a lifetime to say I knew you well..." The truth is that with sex outside of marriage our brains get all gummed up in evaluating the potential of a relationship because of the raging hormones.

Now back to Paul speaking to married couples. "*Do not deprive each other...*" Never use sex as a bribe. The answer is always "yes" if it is at all possible. It is inevitable that one partner wants sex at different times or in different frequencies than the other. If you are not depriving the other it means that the partner who is feeling the desire is the one who is always followed. That is a real partnership.

There is one exception to this that is most interesting. It is not an excuse we might hear today. You might hear, "It's my body and I am saying not tonight." No. No. "*The wife does not have authority over her own body but yields it to her husband. In the same way, the husband does not have authority over his own body but yields it to his wife.*" (1 Corinthians 7:5) "I have a headache" is not an excuse. That is not to suggest that health is not a consideration. The only valid reason requires mutual consent. So let's start there. If you are going to lower the pace of your sex life it must be by mutual consent. This points to a timely truth about Christian marriage. The mutual consent is to suspend your sex life "*so that you may devote yourselves to prayer.*" (1 Corinthians 7:5) Whoever would have guessed that one? When was the last time you didn't have sex because you were devoted to prayer? This implies more than an evening of prayer. It implies that Christian couples are expected to have a mutual prayer life.

The passage goes on. After the season of deprivation because of prayer, "*Then come together again so that Satan will not tempt you because of your lack of self-control.*" (1 Corinthians 7:5) Most people are subject to sexual temptation because Satan knows the carnage he can reap if he gets us to let wandering eyes take over.

God is for good sex. He designed the whole intricate system of body parts and brain chemistry to work to the advantage of every human. It is easy for people to think that by giving into impulses that move them in the wrong direction, those moves will make them happier and more complete. It never works that way. Never. The simple command "*Do not deprive one another...*" (1 Corinthians 7:5) is profound and needs a fair hearing and joyful obedience from everyone in the family of God.

Your Take

1. Where and when do you think it is appropriate to discuss this "*one another*" in connection with church life?
2. Many married partners find it difficult to discuss sex together. Why do you think that is so?
3. How will you overcome your own inhibitions and concerns to discuss sex and live it out righteously in your life?

~ 28 ~

I'm Your Servant

"All of you, clothe yourselves with humility toward one another, because, 'God opposes the proud but shows favor to the humble.'"
(1 Peter 5:5)

If you are impressed with your own humility you are probably not so humble as you think. True humility is not a characteristic of which you are easily aware. Others may see it in you but you will be unaware because it is your new-normal posture.

Wendy's Take

Through the years Gary and I have become acquainted with people who have owned this positive characteristic which I am struggling to define.

I remember Jane who exuded an empathetic warmth and genuine interest in whomever she was talking to. She didn't appear to shed an ounce of self-importance. Her life wasn't on the agenda at that moment. She was not proud even though she and her husband could have been so with their prosperous farming business or from the knowledge they had gained to make their lives successful. Everyone liked being around her with her winsome smile for it gave them a sense of peace. There was no competition. And yet there was no lack of self-esteem but a quiet confidence built within. She didn't have to prove herself to anyone but took on the lowliest task. Maybe I'm painting too perfect a picture of her. You might have to ask her husband or children for the real truth but I don't think it would come out any differently. She was dressed in humility.

Gary's Take

I have taken great comfort and hope from Peter. The man who wrote the two letters toward the end of his life was not the same impetuous, ill-informed and ill-formed man Jesus called. If God can change Peter that much there must be some hope for me!

Humble isn't a word that comes to mind when you hear Peter saying, *"Surely not, Lord!"* (Acts 10:14) Literally translated that is, *"No way, Lord!"* Who is the boss Peter? You or Jesus? How could you be so proud as to contradict Jesus? Actually, Luke records this as a "*voice*" (Acts 10:13, 15) in a "*trance.*" (Acts 10:10) Peter identifies the voice as "*Lord.*" (Acts 10:15) And that isn't the only time he pushed back on Jesus. He wasn't the last man in history to say "Lord" in the same breathe as telling Jesus he isn't Lord!

Then toward the end Peter speaks to all Christians and says, *"All of you clothe yourselves with humility toward one another."* (1 Peter 1:5) There isn't any way to convey this properly in English. The word *"clothe"* has a depth of meaning from a world where up to half the population were slaves. This word has the historical meaning of fastening or tying on a white scarf or apron which distinguished a slave from a freeman. It was a symbol of the status of a slave's servitude. Strap it on people! Strap humility so tightly that in every move you count yourself as the servant and others see you that way as well.

This is not a play acting event when a Christian pretends to be a servant with an unctuous act which, if the truth be known, is designed to impress someone with fake humility.

Perhaps Peter was reflecting on this concept because he had been reading in Proverbs where it says, *"He mocks proud mockers but shows favor to the humble and oppressed."* (Proverbs 3:34) Undoubtedly Peter was embarrassed by the obtuseness he exhibited as recorded in the Gospels. And his own memories of past failings ring down through the centuries as reminders to us.

As a side note, in general terms, the Gospels were written at about the same time or later than Peter himself wrote his letters. The Bible didn't whitewash Peter's early years with revisionist history. The contrast has been wonderfully preserved for us by inspiration.

The famous John Wesley (1791) had a bent for constructing bullet lists of points for people on how to conduct themselves. These were foundational to the Methodist movement that changed the world. Wesley was big on small groups. He insisted they be conducted weekly and start on time. (Not a new problem, huh?) He encouraged transparency among the participants and encouraged them to deal with their own failings, sins and foibles. For example, some of his rules were framed in questions such as, "Do you desire to be told of your faults?" "Do you desire that, in doing this, we should come as close as possible, that we should cut to the quick, and search your heart to the bottom?" It would seem that Wesley knew people needed to be confronted or they would never develop the humility needed for a flourishing Christian life.

We all need to be open to hear what others have to say about us. It takes a good deal of precise self-examination to get this humility thing right and our self-examination needs to be informed. We need to look in the mirror first but we also need others to point out what they see which we missed.

When someone takes the risk to lovingly tell you what they see in you, don't let the sting of that criticism build a wall between you. Don't push your friend away. Do your best to humbly assume their description is correct. At least do so until you have confirmed one way or another whether they are right or wrong. You can ask others if they see the same fault in you. If you don't want others to help you search your heart to the bottom, they won't.

Please note that this strapping on of humility is something for each of us. And it is a one-another characteristic that must permeate our relationships.

In our words and actions we all need a good dose of humility. That starts with modeling by the leaders in every church. When the leaders aren't humble the rest of the people are short of examples to follow. Humility must trickle down from the top if any leader expects it to bubble up from the bottom. At the same time, when humility bubbles up in church from the ordinary people who follow it encourages the leaders to also demonstrate humility in their attitude and manner. Wherever you are in the life of your church let humility be one of the character traits that shines out from you and encourages others to also be humble.

Your Take

1. Do you grimace in your heart when someone brings up an issue they think you need to change? If so, is that because you aren't as humble as you should be? How can you fix that?
2. Where can you improve in your attitudes so that others describe you as humble?
3. Can you imagine the joy and comfort you bring to others if they see you grow in humility? Write your own eulogy as if someone were describing you after you are gone.

~ 29 ~

I've Got This

"Now that I, your Lord and Teacher, have washed your feet, you also should wash one another's feet." (John 13:14)

Jesus taught that the greatest in his kingdom is the one who adopts the lowly position on earth. He explained, "*... whoever wants to become great among you must be your servant, and whoever wants to be first must be your slave – just as the Son of Man did not come to be served, but to serve, and to give his life as a ransom for many.*" (Matthew 20:26-28) This is hard for many Christians to grasp because it is easier to evaluate greatness by a person's media footprint or the size of their ministry or church. We need to recalibrate.

Wendy's Take

I'm sure you would agree that one of the most unpleasant weekly chores in the home is cleaning the toilet. We have two washrooms in our home; so, the work is double. Our teenaged granddaughter just got hired on part-time by her local arena. She is very excited about this opportunity; however, her job list does include cleaning the washrooms. Now, that would be far worse than anyone's domestic challenge. Go for it, Syd!

At one of the churches we attended a few years ago, there was a need for volunteers to clean the washrooms in order to save money. As you can expect not too many volunteers came forward; but an older couple with lots of health issues decided to serve in this way. The upstairs washrooms weren't too bad but the downstairs ones left a little to be desired. Upon entering the women's facility, you had to be careful not to fall down the stairs just after you opened the door. I never did go in there. Being a downtown church, strangers would sneak in to use these rooms leaving them not in the best condition.

I was very impressed with this faithful couple who week after week provided clean washrooms for the rest of the church family to enjoy. Sadly, this lowly task was probably taken for granted without too many thank you's along the way.

Gary's Take

Peter said, "*To this you were called, because Christ suffered for you, leaving you an example, that you should follow in his steps.*" (1 Peter 2:21) Therefore, following Jesus who suffered may involve our own suffering. However, in our key "*one another*" verse Jesus tells us we are to serve one another in a lowly task for his day which was washing feet. In ordinary homes the host provided water and guests washed their own dirty feet presumably as they arrived. In more affluent homes a servant did the job for the guests. When Jesus took the unusual step of getting up during the meal and stripping off his outer clothing to wash feet he did the unthinkable. The basin and the towel apparently were available in the rented room but nobody said, "I've got this." Perhaps Jesus waited to give the Twelve an opportunity to meet the need. We do know what Peter's attitude was to the task based on his response to Jesus. Clearly it had been beneath Peter's dignity to wash feet.

Many believe that when Jesus said, "*Now that I, your Lord and Teacher, have washed your feet, you also should wash one another's feet...*" (John 13:14) that he was speaking literally and many others think he was speaking symbolically. Obviously, there is no functional use to the practice today and to leave it at perfunctory foot washing would miss the point.

Service in lowly ways is not beneath the dignity of any of us if we truly "*follow in his steps.*" (1 Peter 2:21) Then on the other hand, to embarrass others by attempting to serve in an unnecessary way misses the point.

What kind of "foot washing" would be in line for today? There could be many small opportunities and other larger ones as well. We live in Ontario Canada and in the winter an inevitable and unpleasant task from time to time is to clear ice or snow from a car. It is really easy to get out the door first and clear someone's car for them. Foot washing? I think so, because it represents a minor inconvenience to create more comfort for others.

But that is just a start. Taking care of small children for an afternoon gives relief to a young parent who in the moment believes their children will never cease to be a burden.

Raking leaves for a widow who can't bear to move away from the home she shared with her recently departed husband would be a comfort for her. That is true for many other helps one can give to a single person of any age who has basic burdens to bear.

Systemically in the mechanics of church life there are always roles that are less desirable than others. Everyone can set an example by staying late with a young mentee to clean up a mess after a church party.

Home care support is often needed and not always pleasant. Churches often have disabled and semi-disabled people who could use some help. Or moving out one step, the people of the church have other friends, relatives or neighbors who are not connected with the church who could use a loving hand.

Bear in mind a few things about Jesus exemplary teaching in this passage. He washed Judas's feet. And Judas let him. But the passage says, "*For he knew who was going to betray him ...*" (John 13:11) and "*I am not referring to all of you; I know those I have chosen.*" (John 13:18) Jesus showed the same care for Judas as he did for John even though one was easier to love than the other. Neither John nor Judas could do anything to deserve such a demonstration of love.

Jesus jumped up in the middle of the meal. Maybe he smelled stinky feet? He didn't say, "Uh ... could one of you take care of the dusty feet."

Jesus took the initiative. He didn't say, "If any of you would like to have your feet washed the line forms to the left." Or in today's terms, "Text me."

All of this shows us how the Golden Rule – "*So in everything, do to others what you would have them do to you, for this sums up the Law and the Prophets.*" (Matthew 7:12) – only works when you figure out that you are "It!" You have to "do" before they come to you. You have to go get it done before they ask. They might not even know to ask. They can't smell their own stinky feet. Train your sense of smell so that you can.

I have had way too many conversations in my lifetime with people complaining about how nobody cares about them. Then I ask, "Have you known anyone in a circumstance like yours before?" They don't even see this coming. I ask, "So how did you take the initiative to help that person in that similar situation?" They feel like I hit them with a Mac truck. For the first time in their lives they realize that they failed many friends in the past. Honestly, at this exact moment I can't recall anyone saying to me, "I always called them once a week to encourage them." Or, "I took them to the grocery store once a week to help them." Or anything that approximates, "I washed their feet." Not even once, let alone once a week.

Yes, you have to suspend your own agenda to do things like this. You have to have a heart tuned to the stinky feet needs. You have to shut off the tap inside your head that wants to spout out excuses and complaints.

Are you ready to say, "I've got this." more?

Your Take

1. What would you consider to be the lowliest, mundane tasks among the people of your church?
2. Who comes to your mind that has covered this service for many a year? What positive characteristics do they display with their faithfulness? Have you heard them complain about the task?
3. What practical ways can you encourage this person so that they feel worthwhile and loved?

Cool It!

Sometimes you just have to stand back. The problems that seemed so significant a few decades ago probably remain but we have moved on to thinking about more pressing problems. Christians are called to take the long view rather than zig zag across the treacherous landscape of our times. Some things are worth fighting for and some things are not. Some things are also worth waiting for because they have eternity's values in view.

~ 30 ~

Hmmmm Peace

"Salt is good, but if it loses its saltiness, how can you make it salty again? Have salt among yourselves, and be at peace with each other."
(Mark 9:50)

The problems of life can get you down as you well know. And those problems are wide-ranging. Most people take little time to think of the problems elsewhere – in other parts of the globe. Future potential global problems such as over-population, paralyzing poverty, rampant disease, global warming or possible wars don't intersect our day-to-day troubles. It is the problems close to home that unsettle us.

Wendy's Take

I have a problem. I don't understand why the dove has been so connected with the concept of peace – at least not from my backyard. We have a seed station for birds in front of our kitchen window. We only put seed out during the winter months but when we do, various kinds of birds land on the board to peck away at their share. It is interesting to watch their unique habits during our mealtimes. One particular species may congregate together like the sparrows or the doves. Eight doves may be getting along quite nicely but then one new guy will soar in and chase them all away so that he can sit on the pile of seed by himself as king. He can actually get quite nasty. How fair is that and how peaceful is that?

Mark 9:50 records Jesus' words, *"... be at peace with each other."* Throughout our ministry years Gary and I have been involved in, or just visited, churches that are not too peaceful. Similar to this king dove, a leader may want to be front and center by himself, controlling every aspect of the church, not willing to let others take the lead or capable enough to train them for a responsible position. This creates a very unsettling environment with lots of unspoken questions in the minds of the rest of the church members. Is it not important for us to follow Jesus' admonition as best as we can with the Holy Spirit's help so that our church can bear the reputation of peacefulness rather than infighting?

Gary's Take

Jesus told his disciples two important things back to back in this key verse. When he said "... *have salt in yourselves"* he was almost certainly referring to the purifying and preserving nature of salt. He was telling them to mind their own heart business first.

My biggest problems have always been the ones I must control. These are the problems I have between the outer edges of my two ears. The noise in my head is what I must take charge of – no easy task.

The second concept that follows has to do with how we relate to others. That is the one we are focusing on because of the word *"one another"* but the two are like two sides of a coin. If a person won't continually maintain the shine of the one side of that coin – the internal thoughts and feelings – they most certainly won't polish the other side. They won't relate well to others.

Earlier in Mark 9 the childish disciples were having a dispute about who was the greatest. Jesus is speaking, *"'What were you arguing about on the road?' But they kept quiet because on the way they had argued about who was the greatest."* (Mark 9:33) The external argument started in their heads and in their selfishness. The pathetic part of this is that Jesus had just told them he was going to be killed but that he would rise again. They didn't get it at all. But they did get their own selfish desires for the future.

Peace in a church – and it is peace among believers in the church that is the subject – is only possible if we pay attention to it. Circumstances always look a little different from one person's perspective than they do from someone else's. Always. Your own perspective will not be as complete as it should be if you don't learn to look at things from the other person's point of view. Yes, that other person is self-focused – just like everyone else. But you must learn to see how they see to be of any help. Jesus called for a blessed group of peacemakers to emerge. *"Blessed are the peacemakers, for they will be called children of God."* (Matthew 5:9) The child of God has a special role to play in helping people get along.

When a person strives to take over the discussion and assert their own position in such a way as to dominate another into submission there is no potential for true peace. Often that domineering person is misunderstanding what the other person is saying or what they are looking to achieve. The path to peace must be the path on which everyone is open to understanding what the other side needs or wants. Peace is never negotiated by a bully who has to get his own way. It is possible to bully others into submission that might look like peace but it isn't real peace because the buried needs are left unmet. Bullying leads to withdrawal or conflict – not peace.

When you find yourself being stirred up and wanting to argue, take a moment to think about what you really want. It may be that you just want your own way. It is easy enough to select facts, alleged facts and presumed facts to make a skillful argument for a position; it is easy enough to set aside other facts that don't point in your favor. Peace is not a child of exaggeration. When you find yourself wanting to exaggerate or overstate, probably your position isn't as strong as you think. Maybe peace will flow if you simply back off and listen more intently.

Start your pursuit of peace by using your mental powers to imagine yourself in the other person's position. Perhaps there is buried or unfinished business from the past the other person imagines they are defending against. But then perhaps that other person sees something which is a real danger you need to take it into account. Maybe the burden that person is carrying has created an unbearable load that is the genesis of them lashing out. Applying your faculties to discern the possibilities will lead you to inquire. You will do well to ask about the whole picture rather than assuming your tentative arrangement of the facts is the whole story. Once you know what is really going on there is a better chance that you will find the bonding and tranquility at the core of your heart's desire. Perhaps you have to give a little. You always have to give to get. But much more importantly, you as a child of God, called to be a peacemaker, must always draw yourself back to the agenda of the Prince of Peace.

Your Take

1. Who in your church do you find irritating? What are you doing to create a better peaceful arrangement with that person?
2. Are you disposed to setting your own preferences aside in favor of others? Are you willing to do so without merely withdrawing to the sidelines?
3. Where can you take initiative to become a peacemaker for the Kingdom of God?

~ 31 ~

I'll Wait Up

"So then, my brothers and sisters, when you gather to eat, you should all eat together." (1 Corinthians 11:33)

The NIV rendering of 1 Corinthians 11:33 is sensible in the context but it isn't a literal translation. The word for "*one another*" is in there but it doesn't show. The NLT says, *"So, my dear brothers and sisters, when you gather for the Lord's Supper, wait for each other."* That captures the meaning of the whole passage but the "Lord's Supper" part isn't in the original. The purpose of a translation is to convey meaning exchange from one language to another. Both renderings achieve that. A more literal word for word translation is, *"So then brothers of me, coming together in order to eat, one another wait for."* That wouldn't do, would it? You might notice it doesn't say brothers and sisters but it didn't mean males only when it says brothers. You can see what translators are up against in transferring meaning from one language to another. But we can get some really clear instructions about attitudes from this "*one another.*"

Wendy's Take

"Wait your turn!" I used this strong directive often with my pupils as a teacher and with my own children growing up in our home. True enough, curtailing children's enthusiasm as well as their impatience can be a challenge. It is an admired characteristic when good manners have been developed at an early age. Sadly, with all pressures in our society this type of education doesn't always happen.

It is, however, curious to me that 1 Corinthians 11:33 recounts a similar command. Was it really so bad that this comment had to be written down in Scripture?" As we look at our own humanity, truthfully, we all tend to gravitate to this sinful, self-centered nature at times. We go for the best seats at a special event. We become impatient standing in long line-ups or driving through traffic jams when there has been an accident or the weather is poor. Recently, at a funeral we attended, those who lined up first for food at the reception area piled their plates high which didn't leave much left for those at the end of the line. I felt sorry for the grieving family who were quite disappointed with this behavior. Oh my!

Gary's Take

The story from 1 Corinthians 11 gives us solid insight into the imperfect church life in Corinth. It reminds us that no church is what it ought to be in the ideal. But it also reminds us to continue to strive from our real church to a more ideal church.

Here are some of the imperfections from this one chapter.

1. Meetings that did more harm than good. (1 Corinthians 11:17)
2. Divisions in the church. (1 Corinthians 11:18)
3. Making a farce of the Lord's Supper. (1 Corinthians 11:20)
4. Ignoring people. (1 Corinthians 11:21)
5. Letting people go hungry. (1 Corinthians 11:22)
6. Tolerating drunkenness. (1 Corinthians 11:22).
7. Humiliating the less well off. (1 Corinthians 11:23)
8. Net effect of despising the church of God. (1 Corinthians 11:22)

That sounds like a very unattractive church, doesn't it? And there were many other problems Paul calls them out on covered throughout the letter. And yet, the letter is addressed to "*To the church of God in Corinth, to those sanctified in Christ Jesus and called to be his holy people, together with all those everywhere who call on the name of our Lord Jesus Christ–their Lord and ours.*" (1 Corinthians 1:2) That ought to instruct us.

People leave churches because they don't get along with an individual or two. They leave because they find the preaching irritating. They leave because the church won't change fast enough. They leave because they have a falling out with former friends. The list goes on. Rather than digging in and becoming part of the solution they walk away. There may come a time when you must move on from one church to another but Paul's instruction here is worth pondering.

Wait. Wait for people so you can eat the Lord's Supper together. That is the context but it bears extending. Wait for people to institute the change you think they should have implemented earlier.

It might take a month or two, or a year or two for others to come to understand how they should change. It takes time. Sometimes leaders who want things to happen expect change faster than it is possible.

When Wendy and I were in our first full time pastorate after about four years it came time to move on. We believed we had completed all we could do. After we moved on the church went through a solid season of growth. I always figured you could measure the effect of our ministry after we left far better than while we were still there. The church held a lovely farewell event for us to show their appreciation. And that appreciation was genuine and heartfelt. However, I still recall one fine lady whose family had come to the church during our time there saying it was too bad we were moving on so soon because they were just getting to know us. At least from one person's perspective we moved on too soon. It struck me, not that we should have stayed longer, but that it took so long for anything much to change in the hearts and lives of the people. We have fond memories of our years in that village church. Many of those we worked with have since gone on to be with the Lord. But our memories yet remain. They were worth the price and they were worth waiting for.

Wait. There is a saying, "All things come to those who wait." It comes from a poem by Lady Mary Montgomerie Currie who died over a hundred years ago. That phrase sounds hopeful but her poem ends with "They come, but often come too late." So much for that. All good things don't come because you wait but if you don't wait long enough some good result may not materialize. There are many saints who have waited a very long time for results. For example, William Carey, known as the father of modern missions waited seven years before he won his first convert. He did so in the midst of a life of trials. He didn't get on the boat and return to the shoe shop business in England. If he had we wouldn't know his name. The key thing is that he didn't know in year six that waiting a while longer would bring results.

Before you give up on something that sticks to your ribs like a good bowl of porridge consider whether or not you are giving up because you lack sufficient patience. It is stressful to wait for others even if it is just a meal at the church but sometimes waiting is the ingredient that will make all the difference.

Your Take

1. What are you waiting for in your church? What do you do about your feelings of impatience?
2. Have you prayed about the long awaited element missing in your church life? How has that yearning for what is not yet real changed you?
3. Do others see you as an impatient person or one who is willing to wait for others when it is called for to benefit the work of the Lord?

~ 32 ~

I Forgive You

"Bear with each other and forgive one another if any of you has a grievance against someone. Forgive as the Lord forgave you."
(Colossians 3:13, also Ephesians 4:32)

Everyone has many opportunities to forgive over a week let alone a lifetime. You would think that with that much opportunity we would get good at it as naturally as we do up a button or tie a shoe. Not so. Maybe the little offenses are let go but the bigger the expectation the more resentment and bitterness continues to fester. We are quick to say, "*Forgive us our sins*" (Luke 11:4) to our Father. And not so quick to own the next phrase about others who have wronged us with lasting effects.

Wendy's Take

My parents were born in Finland but they spoke Swedish. My independent grandmother decided she wanted to move to Canada in the early 1920s. She packed up herself and her five children, my mother being the eldest at age 14, and began her long journey to the other side of the world. They left behind the culture, the security, the language they knew so well in their homeland. They did not foresee the hard life they would be facing with the onset of a horrible depression in that decade that included a serious lack of employment. My grandfather followed later after loneliness for his family got to him.

The first stopover was England where the two youngest children contracted chicken pox. They had to stay behind for a few weeks with an uncle while the rest of the family sailed for Halifax. My aunt grew to be a very unhappy woman for most of her life probably because of this abandonment, possibly from a moral crisis that occurred in the church she was attending, or maybe it was the early death of her sickly husband whom she dearly loved as well as the death of her second son later on in life. Whatever the cause she had an unforgiving spirit that had developed over those years in relation to others and to God. Regrettably, she refused to forgive and bitterness took over as a result of these hardships with no resolve. It was very difficult to visit her in her 90s in her nursing home as her mind and heart were closed to any spiritual talk. Lack of forgiveness like this among family and church members alike is very prevalent. The repercussions are unfathomable.

Gary's Take

When someone makes a driving mistake that puts you in danger you probably react strongly in the moment. I hope your strong self-preservation instincts don't degenerate into obscene hand gestures or prolonged honking. If you can't find forgiveness in that moment where there is no long term damage you have a problem. Instantaneous anger is not a friend of forgiveness.

But what if the wrong has left you with a permanent scar? What if that driver was impaired and you lost a loved one or a leg? There is permanent blame for the offender. It will always be that driver's fault. At the same time it will always be your responsibility to live with the consequences.

It is hard to imagine in such a hypothetical scenario that the driver got behind the wheel and deliberately thought their impairment was going to end in death or dismemberment. The remote possibility didn't even look like a probability at that moment and definitely not a certainty. Remorse or deflected blame won't eliminate the consequence. And while the pain and memory will remain, forgiveness must enter the equation or the damage will double.

Then there is the hypothetical situation of a driver choosing to take the vehicle and use it as a weapon of mass destruction. We are shocked when it happens and it is hard to fathom such cruelty. It doesn't change anything to find derogatory terms to describe that person. The little baby didn't look like a "monster." The neighbor probably didn't think the driver a "psycho" the day before.

These three levels of offense just illustrated operate in each of our lives to varying degrees on a regular basis. There are inadvertent offenses that seldom leave us with long-term resentment. There are indirect offenses where the offender doesn't intend to leave long term damage. Then there are the intentional acts designed to hurt or destroy.

Forgiveness is not re-framing the offense to a lesser category. This is true even though such a re-categorization from intentional to indirect might be valid. What looks like an intentional action might not have been premeditated. To self-justify people often say, "I'm sorry. I didn't mean it." Whether that is true or not may or may not make a little difference to you. The intentionality doesn't make a whole lot of difference to the consequence.

The validity of the grievance is functionally attached to the feelings of resentment and even rage. However, carrying such feelings on one's shoulders for a long time is a choice unrelated to the grievance or event itself. There is no question that an offense or event might shape one's life going forward whether or not the consequences were intended or unintended. Forgiveness is another matter.

This chapter is only a short reference to forgiveness. And it is easy to point to the need for forgiveness in every situation. However, letting go and moving on instead of allowing bitterness and anger toward others eat away at us might be a battle.

Developing compassion for the offender helps. Taking the long view of life in the future is always a good plan. Talking it out with a trusted counselor or mature Christian confidant may open a valve and let the steam out of your soul. Forgiving yourself because you are forgiven by the Lord is wonderfully freeing.

Holding on to the resentment won't increase the punishment on the offender. Blaming God for what happened puts you in the judge's chair where you simply don't belong.

The instructions in the Book don't supply a lot of detail. They do describe the finish line. *"Forgive as the Lord forgave you."* (Colossians 3:13)

The sooner you find the road to forgiveness – no matter how debilitating the offense – the sooner you will get to a happier and healthier you.

Your Take

1. As you read this chapter did someone you need to forgive come to mind? What is your plan? It won't go away on its own.
2. Do you know an angry, bitter or resentful person in your church? Is there a way you should be getting close to that person to find the blockage and help a brother or sister to wholeness? How will you develop that plan?
3. Do you make it your habit to go back to others to ask for forgiveness when you have wronged them? Describe your feeling before, during and after the event of asking for forgiveness.

~ 33 ~

It's OK

"Be completely humble and gentle; be patient, bearing with one another in love."
(Ephesians 4:2, also Colossians 3:13)

Some people just bug us. You too, huh? It naturally follows that we must bug some others as well. Does that ever occur to you about yourself? The question is, "Why do we irritate each other?" But the better question is, "What can I do to minimize the irritation I feel and cause in others?" When you ask a better question, you are more likely to get a better answer so let's work on that.

Wendy's Take

Is there someone in your church that you regard as being quite obnoxious? One person comes to mind whom I had actually asked to serve on a ministry committee. After attending one meeting this individual agreed to become a team player. After a few more meetings had occurred I realized we were in trouble for when new ideas were presented and accepted by the rest of the group they were not all agreeable to this person. A know-it-all attitude pervaded their whole demeanor. Sometimes comments made were very harsh to others outside of the committee. Inattentive listening happened too often and we learned that financial giving was held back due to lack of acceptance of what the church leadership was trying or not trying to accomplish.

I was getting rather discouraged with my list of growing judgments and decided to dig deeper for some positivity because of the New Testament exhortation to forbear or show tolerance for one another. (Just a sidebar – Gary was laughing one Sunday when exiting the parking lot of a large church. He had let four cars go ahead of him and the person behind him honked at him to get going. No forbearance there!) I believe our friend really wanted what was best for our particular ministry and for the church as a whole but perhaps needed a different role. Faithfulness and responsibility showed up when asked to help run a sub-committee of the group. Intentional hospitality was a key factor in their home for numerous church people were invited over for dinner. Even though I did confront some of the obnoxiousness, my change of attitude helped me to cope with this developing relationship for the good of all.

Gary's Take

It is possible to be irritated by someone and still not sin. We know that because Jesus, who was sinless, was irritated by the unbelieving people around him, "*'You unbelieving and perverse generation,' Jesus replied, 'how long shall I stay with you? How long shall I put up with you?'*" (Matthew 17:17) The stimulus was the lack of faith that Jesus could heal a little boy. By then they should have known better. The disciples, with the greater exercise of faith, could have done the job themselves.

Incompetence is irritating when competence should reasonably be expected. Immature attitudes in others might drive you nuts. However, we all drop the ball from time to time. It is easy to notice the other person's failure and harder to admit our own. This whole book probably is a great reminder to you that you can do better in your relationships with one another.

The key here is that we are instructed to bear with each other. In spite of the failures of others we are required by the Lord to live out equanimity. Equanimity is mental calmness, composure, and evenness of temper, especially in difficult situations. The concept is that we must stand erect and firm sustaining our composure and demeanor in spite of the disquieting behavior of others. Be careful to make the distinction here. It is not wrong to feel and even express frustration at appropriate times; it is wrong to let that frustration take you into a course of action that violates the standards you ought to be living by.

This quality of forbearance is to be exhibited by all. But get used to it; it won't be. You have to be the adult in the room even when the others are squabbling liked spoiled children. In the moment, when emotions are running high you have to choose appropriate behavior.

Appropriate behavior isn't always just to let things go. Remember how Jesus flipped the tables? My father on occasion used the phrase, "It's time to read the riot act!" I knew a severe reprimand was coming. Actually, The Riot Act was an Act of the Parliament of Great Britain that authorized local authorities to declare any group of twelve or more people to be unlawfully assembled, and thus have to disperse or face punitive action. The act, whose long title was "An Act for preventing tumults and riotous assemblies, and for the more speedy and effectual punishing the rioters", came into force on August 1, 1715. (Thank you Wikipedia.)

Forbearance doesn't mean that we put up with bad behavior. It does mean that we carefully evaluate what is going on when we feel the temperature rising and we feel compelled to blurt out words we might later regret. One event isn't likely to stick in our memory but a repeated offense causes our temperature to rise. We need a strategy to keep from messing things up more than they are.

The first step to develop a forbearing attitude is analysis. It is not reasonable to expect a person to behave in a certain way if they don't know what is required. Some people come from what we might call a rough background. Their minds are all messed up because of their upbringing. It will take some time for the grace of God to infiltrate the inner recesses of their soul. If there is evidence of sincerity and general progress cut some people some slack. You can't bolt a mature Christian head on an immature Christian who is on the road to greater sanctification.

The second step is reflection. Take some quiet time to think about how you are going to *"... bear with one another in love."* (Ephesians 4:2) Love isn't primarily a warm emotion; it is a readiness to sacrifice one's own agenda and self in favor of the other person's need. Set aside your own selfishness and preferences first and then your heart might warm up a little.

The final step is action. It is always more about how you act than it is about what you know or believe. Read the book of James and get a siren reminder about that. Forbearance will surely follow.

Your Take

1. Make a list of all the people in your church you have trouble forbearing. What is your approach to them? How do you keep yourself from just avoiding them?

2. What evidence is there that you are bugging people in your church from time to time? What can you do to make it easier for others to tolerate you?
3. When you see a church fight brewing, what proactive steps do you take to help ward off the disaster?

~ 34 ~

It's Not All About Me

"Let us not become conceited, provoking and envying each other."
(Galatians 5:26)

These negative characteristics of conceit, provocation and envy are all too common. They need our attention or we will never get them stopped. That is why the Holy Spirit inspired the words to draw our attention to them. So let's dig in.

Wendy's Take

Have you ever watched toddlers provoking their siblings or playmates? They can be really sneaky even at that early age in getting their own way. If one child seizes a favorite toy, another will come along and grab it away. The shrill screaming begins that won't stop until the parents step in and put them in "time out." The children come back all repentant and a whispered apology might be heard if you listen closely depending upon how persistent the parents are at gaining that required response.

In church life there are many different kinds of people that can provoke me or "get my goat!" There are the arrogant ones – those who display a "know-it-all" attitude even when they can't see the whole church picture or refuse to consider a different viewpoint; the bullies – those who must put others down to make themselves look good or maintain control at all costs; and the picky people – those who want their own way and will leave the church if they don't get it. Have you ever noticed that these conflicts particularly rise up when a church is reaching out intentionally and effectively to their community with the Gospel message or if they find themselves in the midst of a building program with all the stress of decision-making that has to occur? It's a wonder my tongue isn't half its size because of biting down on it through the half century of our ministry. Sadly, it is quite infrequent that any of these followers of Christ come back and apologize for their self-centered behavior.

Gary's Take

One of the lofty passages of Scripture Christians ought to know and quote is Galatians 5:22-23 where the bullet point list of the aspects of the fruit of the Spirit are itemized. But we also should see exactly what follows that list. Paul explains that all Christians are those who have crucified the flesh with its passions and desires. Kill that old nature. You did it, did you not? If not you don't qualify as one who belongs to Christ. Look it up if you don't believe me. (Galatians 5:24) Then Paul talks about attitudes that could creep in. It is possible to become something we ought not to become. That is what Galatians 5:26 teaches.

It is possible to lose our way. Paul warns us of that. It is possible to become conceited, provoking and envying each other. In another chapter we will look more specifically at envying.

Now let's face this provoking thing. The word means "to challenge or enter into a contest with another thus irritating them." Do you find yourself feeling uncomfortable when another person comes up with an idea the group likes better than your idea? And then do you fight back? Ahhh, provoking. You don't always have to be right, you know. Even if the person with the other idea is in some way your junior or subordinate, it isn't a threat to you when they do better than you. It isn't all about you. It is about a fully functioning church where all the *"one anothers"* are on plain display.

The psychological word that applies here is "narcissism." You can Google that to gain a deeper understanding. The word refers to a tendency to think that your ideas are always better; your talents are always superior. Thus a narcissist can't stand it when someone else gets the attention. The universe is out of kilter to them if they are not the center of attention. Narcissists can't distinguish between an attack on themselves and an idea external to themselves.

Further, narcissists always see life as a competition in which they must prevail. They firmly believe everyone else in the room is just like them and wants to get to the center of things.

Narcissists seek out occupations where they can be admired and paid attention to. Those who are in pastoral ministry are often there in part because they have strong narcissistic tendencies. In its full-blown state narcissism is categorized as a personality disorder. So to paraphrase an old children's song, that references eyes, ears, hands, feet and mouth, "Oh be careful little heart what you think. There's a Father up above and He's looking down in love. Oh be careful little heart what you think." Narcissists are tedious because they think they have the right to be right and in charge. To the narcissist, he wouldn't be so domineering if he weren't right. It seldom occurs to him that he might be wrong. And if he is proven to be wrong it will be a rare event for him to admit it or apologize as Wendy has pointed out.

You no doubt see that it is the conceited ones who become the great provokers. They challenge almost every idea with their own better idea unless the idea seems too small to fight over.

The provoker becomes a master debater at putting their own ideas in the center of the table. Even when the idea is rejected by a group they keep coming back to it over and over. They just can't drop it. They wait their turn until they can pounce again. The people around them hide their irritation because they want to be nice. Thus the dominating provoker thinks, since after all he is the superior intellect in the room, that he has won the crowd to his view which of course is the correct view in his opinion. He is satisfied; everyone else masks their discouragement.

It is seldom a good idea to confront the provoker in front of others. That only ups the ante in the grand competition the provoker truly believes he is in. However, if you take him aside and firmly but warmly describe to him what others are thinking or saying behind his back you might get him to back off. Might.

And if you suspect you might be a provoker remember a couple of things. You can only see the truth if you entertain the concept that others might be right. You can always ask your trusted confidants if you are pushing too hard. But then, provokers often don't have anyone to go to. That in itself is a sign you might be the one. You could be in an evolution you never recognize because Paul uses the word "become." That means, to emerge or transition from one condition to another. The habit of provoking grows if you let it. So stop it right now.

Your Take

1. Who is your great nemesis in your church? You might think of that person as the provoker. However, does that person count you as the provoker?
2. How much time have you invested in developing self-understanding no matter how painful that may be?
3. Do you keep your emotional reactions in check so that you can evaluate ideas objectively?

Stop It!

These things must be eliminated. There are no ifs, ands or buts. You might not even know they are characteristic of your interaction with others unless you pay close attention. Others aren't as likely as they could be to help you see the things that are hurting your relationships. So you had better pay close attention.

~ 35 ~

That Hurts

"If you bite and devour each other, watch out or you will be destroyed by each other." (Galatians 5:15)

Have you ever been bitten by an animal? Gary has been attacked by two dogs in his life. The other day our daughter's cat bit Wendy's finger. She thought she was patting him gently. These incidents are often unexpectedly shocking and painful. But biting words are worse.

Wendy's Take

In one of the churches we served at, an elderly lady had operated a library/bookstore for about 30 years. This ministry had lost its usefulness and she was considering giving up her position. Her room was needed for an additional staff member and so the board had decided that the shelves and books were to be moved to a portion of the church sanctuary not being used. I had called her a few days before this change and she seemed fine with the idea. On the following Sunday morning I was in this room to take some of the books to the new location. She came in and all of a sudden started ranting on how the leaders of the church always seemed to get their own way. A couple of her friends that happened to be there as well tried to console her. In all our years of ministry no one had ever confronted me like this so it was rather upsetting. I guess she found it really hard to give up control of her passion.

A couple of weeks later she came to me before a seniors meeting and began to apologize. I gratefully accepted her apology and we hugged. She was courageous enough to make things right. Then I scooted down the hall to

Gary's office in tears. He saw that I was upset and asked if I was sick. I told him no but that this lady had apologized and it meant a great deal to me. After this episode we were able to be friendly with each other. What a wonderful relief and blessing.

Gary's Take

If you might be sorry you said it later then don't say it in the first place. Sounds simple enough but biting words sneak out. Some say it is about having a good filter. I'm not so sure that is the whole solution. Jesus said, *"For the mouth speaks what the heart is full of."* (Matthew 12:34) It is not about filtering out what you want to say; it is about what is in your heart in the first place.

When you get bitten with words you probably form your own retorts in your heart. Like children fighting in the school yard you say to yourself, "Oh yeah. Oh yeah? Well let me tell you what I think about you. I know I'm not so perfect but neither are you!" Really? What does that add to the discussion? How would blurting those words out loud move a needed reconciliation forward? How does pointing out the fault of the other person in this context help? When did counter-punching ever achieve anything good? Paul was very clear. If you bite and devour you destroy each other. Don't do that.

We all have heart disease. The only antidote to a growling heart that is ready to bite when bitten is to fix the heart with the salve of love. Here is the whole thought from Paul. *"For the entire law is fulfilled in keeping this one command: 'Love your neighbor as yourself.' If you bite and devour each other, watch out or you will be destroyed by each other."* (Galatians 5:14-15)

Back to the schoolyard. What is going on when you defend yourself by telling the other person how bad they are too? Folks, probably that is not new information. In fact, the reason for biting words to you is a chain reaction from them having been bitten by someone or some situation themselves. Bitter biting never relieves or heals a wound in yourself or in the other person.

You won't fix anyone else by giving them a piece of your mind you can ill afford to lose. Change your mind first. Ask yourself how you yearn to be loved. What self-donation or self-sacrifice could others make that would move your life up a notch? That is how you want to be loved. So do as you are told. It sums up the whole law. *"Love your neighbor as you love your-*

self." (Matthew 22:39) Go ahead and love yourself by wishing others could see the love you long for. But then redirect your perception of how true love works and give it to the other person – that neighbor.

It is not an option; it is a command. So always be quick to ask yourself, "What does love demand I do?" That other person is carrying a heavy load too. It is just a different load than yours. Seek to understand the other person's need and meet that need with loving words and actions.

When you take the time to get to know someone you understand more about how their personality was formed. You really can't know a person through one conversation. It takes time. Before you attempt to help the other person with their biting words, do your best to help them find out how they think. They might believe their biting words are called for when they are not. Find out how they think so that you know the reasons behind what they say.

There is a time for loving rebuke or correction. It is never the right time to correct the other person based on the personal pain you are feeling. Fill your own heart with waves of forgiveness until your own pain washes away. The memory of the bite will leave a scar and you won't forget easily. But you can recall the bite without reliving the pain every time you think of it. When you tell the story again to yourself and you feel the embers start to glow brighter and even burst into flames you are certainly not ready to fix the other guy. You are likely to use words that you think are well-chosen but come across like you are using a flamethrower. Not a good plan!

Biting and devouring leads to destruction. Mulling over how good it would feel to put the other person in their place won't fix your own heart. Your job on this planet is not to run around like a dog catcher finding the biting dogs. It is really plain. Learn from how others bite and do the opposite.

Your Take

1. When was the last biting sentence or speech you heard that hurt you? Why do you let yourself keep thinking about it?
2. When was the last time you saw a church disagreement with biting words? Did you jump in to lower the tension and help in reconciling the two parties?
3. How can you invest time imagining yourself as a peacemaker? James

said, “Peacemakers who sow in peace reap a harvest of righteousness.” (James 3:18) How is your harvest coming along?

~ 36 ~

Don't Lie

"Do not lie to each other, since you have taken off your old self with its practices and have put on the new self, which is being renewed in knowledge in the image of its Creator." (Colossians 3:9-10)

There is no area of life where lies don't mess us all up. There are lies in the home, in the workplace, in commerce, in politics and everywhere else. Sadly, there are lies in church and so we need the admonition to get the lies out of our lives.

Wendy's Take

Nothing steamed me more as a parent when our four children growing up in our home would lie to us or knowingly neglect to tell us important information that we should be informed about. Thankfully that didn't happen very often. The eldest advising the younger ones to 'fess up before it didn't turn into a very pretty picture for them probably helped them along the way if they heeded her advice.

As a school teacher it always upset me when I had to confront a child when caught in the act of lying. It did help when I considered the background this child was coming from. Maybe his parents were not giving him enough proper attention. Maybe they did not value the benefit of telling the truth. It's not new that one lie usually leads to the necessity of telling another lie. Or maybe these parents were looking up to ambitious political or company leaders who are probably not the best examples to follow. It greatly astounds us when these leaders are caught in acts of deception – deception that appears to be more prevalent now than many other times in history or it could be we just hear about it sooner due to so much media focus.

Similarly it is extremely disconcerting to me when church family members are caught lying about an issue or at least some how prevaricating the truth for their own gain. It can just be not fulfilling a simple responsibility that they promised they would take care of with many others relying on them. After understanding the situation better it is still very difficult to give back full respect to that person as one of God's children. You are just not sure whether or not to trust that person again.

Gary's Take

So we all tell lies. Can we agree on that? If not, maybe we need to work on what a lie actually is.

When we argue black is white it is clear we are lying if we know the difference between black and white. Either you are telling the truth or you are not. But that doesn't exhaust the subject.

You remember when something went wrong in your family the most responsible child was "Not Me." And every one of the siblings protested "Not Me." Somebody wasn't telling the truth. But in the moment the guilty person found some justification to claim innocence. That is because all people have an ability to use "motivated reasoning." That is a technical term and you can look it up. Without getting technical, the concept is that we select facts or allege facts to argue for the outcome we want in the first place. We can do back flips to create the outcome we desire. In the case of "Not Me" we simply didn't want the punishment and so claimed justifications such as, "He started it!"

We are all capable of self-justifications which are built on half-truths or even untruths. We can even talk ourselves into falsehoods. We lie to ourselves. It is remarkable how much we are wired by our old nature to wiggle out of responsibility. Never doubt that your personal capacity to play such mental games is very much in tact. It is no game. It is sin.

We might first lie to ourselves and then perpetuate those lies with others. They seem like lesser lies if we can get ourselves to believe them first before we tell others the lies.

Collective lies are devastating. Church leaders have often withheld truth that needs to be shared with the people of their church. That amounts to a lie because it creates the same end result as a lie. For example, if a church is building an addition but doesn't want the sticker shock to be too great, it is tempting to leave out the cost of furniture for the addition. Only the sharpest eye will look at the budget and notice the omission. Really, isn't that just lying to knowingly leave out or understate the numbers?

When you err on the side of full disclosure you minimize the possibility that someone will accuse you of lying. People want to know the whole truth that needs to be known to make wise decisions.

The leaders in a church must lead by example. When they attempt to manage information by keeping the truth that should be known from the rest of the church, they create distrust. Lack of trust is hard to restore once the trust has been broken. Instead of keeping information from people that will impact their choices, simply tell the truth. Never hope that difficult facts will go away on their own or be left undiscovered.

You might not like the strong word "lie" and prefer another word such as "perspective." But when a lie is a lie it isn't a matter of perspective.

Stop it. That is what Paul said, *"Do not lie to one another."* (Colossians 3:9) Don't minimize the impact of your self-deceptions. Don't re-suit yourself up with your old self you have taken off and thus reject the process of putting on the new self.

Sometimes it is a lie to allow others to believe something that isn't true when you know otherwise. Sometimes it is a lie to hide what someone is doing because you falsely believe that the cause of Christ would be hurt if you exposed the truth. Sometimes it is a lie to leave people with the wrong impression which you could correct. Sometimes it is a lie to fail to point out a deficiency. You have to live with your own conscience on many matters. Enliven your conscience. You can do so by always asking yourself some serious questions such as, "If they knew what I know, would it change their decision?" and "Am I telling the truth, the whole truth and nothing but the truth?"

Lying is a characteristic of the old nature. It has no part in a sanctified Christian life. Become a trusted example by learning to be a straight shooter who doesn't cover up what needs to be exposed.

Your Take

1. Do I have a habit of living out lies by hiding truth from others? What will I do to enhance my resolve to live in the truth?
2. Where in our church are we lying to ourselves about our true allegiances? How will I be a catalyst to demonstrate that Jesus is Lord of my whole life?
3. Do you have a resolve to confront lies when you hear them? What methods do you use to get at the truth without creating more damage than the exposure of the lie would be worth?

~ 37 ~

Don't Judge

"Therefore let us stop passing judgment on one another. Instead, make up your mind not to put any stumbling block or obstacle in the way of a brother or sister.." (Romans 14:13)

You have heard others say we should never judge others. It is true that the Judge is Jesus and our role is to lean into acceptance. At the same time, Jesus taught us that we could know people by their fruit. So that makes us fruit inspectors. It is one thing to have a different opinion than another person but quite another to diminish our regard of the person who thinks differently. We need to have a healthy approach to our differences.

Wendy's Take

Gary and I book monthly appointments with our chiropractor to keep our bodies in the best alignment for better health. Others may judge us by saying we are wasting our money. Oh well, perhaps they haven't given chiropractic a good try!

Our current chiropractor is very personable. He always seems to enjoy hearing about our latest activities. Last month we explained that we were coauthoring a book on the term "*one anothering*." It took him a few minutes to understand what we were talking about as he had never thought about the idea before. Then he commented, "I guess it's like me taking the garbage out and my wife not really understanding what is going on unless she does it sometime herself." Maybe she had judged him complaining about why this chore took so long.

Likewise in the church there is much judging of other church members in how they are performing their works of service. It is extremely positive and life changing when one person wears another person's shoes. That person can come back and exclaim, "I never realized how hard it is to teach a Sunday School class before now!" Another might gain an entirely different perspective when volunteering to help with a special youth event, particularly when their own teenagers are involved. Or how about a dad taking care of a screaming baby in the nursery for the first time? Judging one another comes too easy; supporting one another becomes very enlightening.

Gary's Take

It is really easy to see what the athlete should be doing when watching a big screen from an armchair. Perhaps that is why people are so obsessed with sports. No sweat; no bruises; just a fine tuned ability to talk to the screen and coach in fantasy.

I like this quote from President Theodore Roosevelt from over a hundred years ago. "It is not the critic who counts; not the man who points out how the strong man stumbles, or where the doer of deeds could have done them better. The credit belongs to the man who is actually in the arena, whose face is marred by dust and sweat and blood; who strives valiantly; who errs, who comes short again and again, because there is no effort without error and shortcoming; but who does actually strive to do the deeds; who knows great enthusiasms, the great devotions; who spends himself in a worthy cause; who at the best knows in the end the triumph of high achievement, and who at the worst, if he fails, at least fails while daring greatly, so that his place shall never be with those cold and timid souls who neither know victory nor defeat." I don't know much about Roosevelt, his life or his career. I do know he was onto something that should be applied in every context – especially in the church.

It is the people who are willing to try and fail who ultimately try again and win. It is much easier to critique someone on why their effort or idea was unsuccessful. But it is very easy to put a stumbling block in the way of someone who is making honest effort. Such a stumbling block will discourage the person from trying again the next time.

We all have limited brain power. It is amazing power beyond our comprehension but still limited. We can learn from others if we choose to. But we are wasting our capacity if we apply an inordinate amount to figuring out what the other person is doing wrong. Take a look at the people you judge to be failing and don't do what they do. It is really simple.

You might gain some short term emotional boost by judging other people. You will always be able to find people living a less useful life than you are. If that is the boost you want you are moving in the wrong direction. You will likely become more and more like the people you are judging.

There is an alternative. Whenever you think it is time to dwell on the failings of others make up your mind to take a different approach. Paul explains it clearly. *"... make up your mind not to put any stumbling block or obstacle in the way of a brother or sister,"* (Romans 14:13) This is a choice. You can choose to shut the judge in you down and apply the same brain power to a different activity.

Don't put a boulder in any other person's path. Here are some practical things to do instead of judging. Be an example. Be early. If you arrive late you give others the permission to arrive late. Wear a smile and enthusiastic tone of voice. Talk to more people. If you don't talk to people you give others permission to keep to themselves. If you don't invite people to your house they may never learn the joy of hospitality. When you talk to people accentuate the positive. Simply use the word "and" more than you use the word "but" in your conversations. The word "but" could lead people to believe you are about to reject their ideas.

In short, if you don't live out the *"one anothers"* described in this book you will by your non-performance be setting the negative example for others to not take the change the Gospel supplies seriously.

You don't have time to judge others. Work hard at finding ways to inspire yourself to do better next time. You have too much work to do on you than you have time to figure out what is wrong with someone else.

Your Take

1. As you think of your inner dialogue, how much of it have you devoted to figuring out what is wrong with others? How can you move your attention to removing stumbling blocks?
2. How does it make you feel when you leave a conversation where the focus has been on some other person's failures? What do you do to keep

yourself from becoming a major contributor to the discouragement of others?

3. What do you do when you see someone trapped in a sin? Do you hide behind the concept of avoiding judgment or do you take steps to help? What are those steps?

~ 38 ~

Careful Now

"Brothers and sisters, do not slander one another. Anyone who speaks against a brother or sister or judges them speaks against the law and judges it. When you judge the law, you are not keeping it, but sitting in judgment on it." (James 4:11)

Slander today is a legal term. It means, "the action or crime of making a false spoken statement damaging to a person's reputation." But for James this concept is far more expansive than what one might say while lying about another person or their performance. This too, gives us meaty food for thought.

Wendy's Take

Blue Jays love coming to the seed station in our backyard to snag their favorite peanuts. They are beautifully dressed. The color of their feathers reminds me of the clear, turquoise waters along the magnificent shores of Georgian Bay, Ontario where Gary and I recently visited with my sister. However, when these Jays fly in all of sudden onto the board with their strident screech, it sounds like they are slandering the other birds that are there enjoying their own feast of seeds. How upsetting is that! There's lots of flapping of wings as they take off in every direction as fast as possible.

When slander arises in a church, as it must have in the New Testament according to James 4:11, an upsetting scenario results which can cause much hurt with the ensuing flapping of tongues. A person dressed beautifully like the Blue Jay on the outside may not be able to unexpectedly control their tongue regarding another which exposes a not so beautiful heart on their inside. Is part of it due to jealousy or insecurity? Whatever the cause James exhorts us not to do that. Bye, bye Blue Jay! We don't want to be around you when your condemning slander appears.

Gary's Take

Slander is probably as close as you can come to directly translate the Greek word James uses three times in one verse. In our day we think of slander as making false and/or damaging statements about another person. This is bad enough that there are laws against deliberately doing it. But for James this isn't a legal matter.

The word deserves some nuanced explanation. It comes from two Greek words stuck together. The two words are "down" and "to speak." This word for "to speak" is often used with the idea of chatter. We might speak of it as letting our inner voice come out of our mouths unadvisedly. When we add the concept of "down" to that we get the idea of letting our inner evil twin rattle away to make less of someone. Think road rage. When you are alone in your car you can mutter all sorts of things about the other driver and her (his?) lack of courtesy or driving skills. You might not be willing to repeat what you say to his (her?) face. Or at least you would measure your tone more carefully.

When the design of your words is to help someone have a lowered opinion of another you are slandering. You will never rise higher by trying to take someone else down. So why bother letting that inside voice get to your outer voice?

We all have negative characteristics. If you can't recall someone pointing that out to you, you probably haven't been listening. And if we don't listen, we won't have the opportunity to improve. If we don't take those words to heart and evaluate any needed change then we won't grow.

Slander isn't about frank feedback; it is about a deliberate attempt to lower someone's opinion of another when there is no warrant for a warning.

When people get close to one another they see behind the veneer of the public interface of the personality and see some of the hidden blemishes. Therefore, as we get closer to the nice people in our church we will probably find out they aren't as nice as we once thought. That is inevitable.

The truth of our fallen humanity often becomes a burden to new believers who falsely think that mature Christians have reached a state of perfection. After about six months new people in a church re-evaluate their participation and ask themselves the question, "Are my new friends here better than my old friends I left behind?" If the answer is negative they will wander back to their old ways. Therefore, it is important to the health and growth of your church that everyone is careful to speak the truths that will build people up and not tear them down.

James 4 is a hard-hitting chapter. As you read it you can almost hear the tension in James' voice as he takes us to school about our sinful nature. He rebukes the Christians of his day for several faults and wrong attitudes. His instruction extends to us. He wasn't suggesting that we all sit around holding hands singing camp songs by the fire. He is warning us in very strong terms about the potential of sin in our lives. He calls us to repent because enough of us need serious change.

When we experience the discovery that people are imperfect, how should we respond? It makes no sense to spread the bad news far and wide. And on the other hand, it makes no sense to let someone perpetuate a hypocrisy before the world. In extreme cases it takes a thoughtful and prayerful intervention. The rest of the time it takes a warm-hearted acceptance that your friend is on a journey of development just like us all.

In a more general way, there is a time to explain aspects of the fallenness of humanity so that others will learn to understand and not become disillusioned. Heroes often aren't as heroic as first thought after all. Peter said, *".. love each other deeply, because love covers over a multitude of sins."* (1 Peter 4:8) It will never help to prattle on about the failings of others. Venting won't change anything.

Perhaps there is someone in your world who looks great on the outside but underneath it all is a screeching blue jay. The best thing to do is figure out the inner need that person is experiencing and then search for a way to help the person to a higher level. You are not the best judge of what is really going on and so be careful with what comes out of your mouth. What you really need is an insightful voice that speaks to the solutions not the description of the problems.

Your Take

1. When you find yourself wanting to tell the truth about someone that the other person doesn't need to know, how do you keep from shooting your mouth off?
2. To what degree does your own envy drive you to wanting to bring someone else down because others think more of them than they should? How much do you really evaluate your own motives before speaking up?
3. What do you do when you sense that someone is slandering another? What words do you use to turn the conversation into a more helpful direction?

~ 39 ~
Oh Stop It

"Don't grumble against one another, brothers and sisters, or you will be judged. The Judge is standing at the door!" (James 5:9)

Nobody wants to be judged by others. But how much concern do we place on being judged by the real Judge? Grumbling about your fellow believers is one sure fire way to stir up the Judge. Not a good plan.

Wendy's Take

Do you like being around people who grumble all the time? I certainly don't. Their negative attitude is very discouraging and depressing. Their list of complaints is tall – money, health, government, church, relatives, house, car, friends etc. Nothing seems right for them in their world. Studies have shown that if a person grumbles a lot in their younger years, their grumbling will get worse the older they become. Positive compliments always carry more weight.

Grumbling and complaining has no place in church life according to James 5:9. I remember one particular business meeting at a church Gary was pastoring. An important discussion about purchasing land for the church to build on was probably on the table. Dan, a church member stood up and began criticizing Gary for his leadership which left a bad taste in the atmosphere of the meeting. He compared Gary to Jimmy Jones which was quite an insult. According to Wikipedia, we learn, "James Warren Jones was an American religious and cult leader, who initiated, and was responsible for a mass suicide and mass murder in Jonestown, Guyana in 1978. He believed communism was the correct social order, in compliance with God's will." Dan was known for not getting along with others. He had moved his family over and over again due to employment changes. Years later after moving out west he and his wife visited our church. He told Gary that he was the best pastor he had ever had. Go figure!

Gary's Take

I admit it. I grumble sometimes. It doesn't get me very far but I do it anyway. "Why?" That is a hard question to answer. But a more important question is, "Why do I do that when the Bible explicitly tells me not to?" The only conclusion I can draw is that grumbling is sin. Perhaps it is the sin that is tolerated most in church life. We need to look at this carefully to eliminate it.

Note that James is talking about grumbling or complaining about each other in the church. When the pastor complains about the people it creates a culture where in turn the people complain about the pastor. The pastor is usually the one with the public voice and can apply its power to generically complain about people. It is really easy for a preacher to try to get at one or two people by fitting it into a sermon under the guise of an appropriate biblical rebuke. If you are a pastor bear in mind that the only public rebuke authorized in the New Testament is the reproving of an elder (pastor) who is sinning.

There is a time to notice when another is failing and bring exhortation to that person. None of us can see all the flaws in our own behavior without the help of another believer pointing them out to us. We need constructive criticism. Grumbling about someone is very different. When a person grumbles about another it is usually because they are trying to build an opposition coalition against someone. While there may be time for a group intervention, that should only be true as a resort after repeated direct explanation to the person by multiple individuals on an individual basis. If you have a complaint to bring about a person, bring it to their face, not behind their back.

When any believer grumbles behind another's back it is a misdemeanor that brings judgment. And as James explains, the Judge is right there at your door.

There are times when you need to discuss how to overcome negative attitudes and behaviors in others. Solution-focused discussion is designed to build people up. Grumbling is designed to tear people down.

Paul tells us, *"Do everything without grumbling or arguing."* (Philippians 2:14) The word used here for grumbling actually means muttering under your breath. This refers to secret displeasure not openly discussed. This is about the committee in your head. We all have a committee in our head. We have confusing voices and thoughts. Our thoughts are the basis of what we choose to do. Therefore, when we have a committee member in our head who has bad ideas we need to shut him/her up. If we don't quell that voice it could turn into some very bad choices. It may seem like a pleasurable event to listen to a negative voice for a while. After all we can tell ourselves it is just a fantasy. No, actually that fantasy in the heart is another separate evil. Tell that committee member to leave the room. You are the chairperson of your committee in your head and you must maintain control of the discussion before it breaks out in a donnybrook.

Then there are circumstances to complain about. James isn't talking about that but such complaining also comes into the picture. Paul might be referring to circumstances because he uses the all-encompassing word "everything." You have probably heard about Murphy's Law. "Anything that can go wrong will go wrong." Then there is Finagle's Corollary. "Anything that can go wrong will go wrong – at the worst possible moment." There are days when both these mythical guys seem like optimists! I don't have to explain to you how this all works. Things break. You hit unexpected walls. Weather happens. Dirt appears out of nowhere. You make mistakes and have do overs. You can add to the list. And you know that going forward life is going to be the same. Things just don't always work out. This compounds the unrealistic premise that others aren't supposed to mess up.

In all these circumstances the correct response is to apply thankfulness. Paul tells us so. *"In every thing give thanks: for this is the will of God in Christ Jesus concerning you."* (1 Thessalonians 5:18)

So for all you grumblers out there give yourself a shake and quit the grumbling. Oh wait. I admitted I can be one of that group. I needed this for me today as I face some unforeseen circumstances. Again. This world would be a much better place if I were a much better man. Will you join me in this self-improvement course?

Your Take

1. Does anyone ever tell you to stop grumbling? How often and when? Do you see a pattern.
2. Are you conscious of the committee in your head? What do you do to take control of the grumbling members?
3. How much do you look at others and find things to complain about them? What can you do to change that bad habit?

~ 40 ~

It's Easy Being Green

"Let us not become conceited, provoking and envying each other."
(Galatians 5:26)

Envy sneaks up on you if you are not careful. Shakespeare popularized associating green with envy with this line, "Beware, my lord, of jealousy; it is the green-eyed monster which doth mock the meat it feeds on." Envy is a yucky feeling aroused by observing another person's apparent better situation. It could be their possessions, qualities or apparent good fortunes you wish were your own that you choose to resent. Be assured that envy will never enhance your own life.

Wendy's Take

Don't you love watching an artist draw a picture? Our daughter, Rebekah, is known as an artist in Kelowna, British Columbia where she and her family reside. Many there might be envious of her talent. I might be envious too as I can't draw a straight line and neither can her father. But I also know that she has put in her 10,000 hours to develop this improving skill. She has created art over and over again since pre-school days. She has learned new artistic techniques plus using different mediums and by studying famous artists from the past. She has taken her creative bent and unwavering pursuit to new heights over the years because she wanted to and surrounded herself with others who wanted to do the same.

Our churches are filled with talented people. They can sing, play an instrument, speak, perform and teach exceedingly well. As with Rebekah they too have put in their 10,000 hours to advance their abilities and build up their confidence. Others envy them and moan that they could never accomplish what their eyes see and their ears hear. Those people need to give themselves a shake and seek out where their passion and capabilities lie for God has given everyone their own special gifts and talents to be used for his glory. In his family there is no excuse for laziness or a lack of self-confidence.

Gary's Take

Envy is the seedbed of a lot of evil. It is a duplicitous, guileful place. It is out of envy that people say one thing, which may be convincing on the surface, to describe another person or situation when the truth is quite another set of facts. For example, one leader in a church might suggest another person isn't ready yet to take on a role or responsibility when in reality the leader fears that person might be quite successful and supplant their own preferences. Putting one person down will never build another person up.

There is always a place for more than one good idea. Jealousy that your own idea isn't the first one picked doesn't mean that your idea won't get its chance in due course.

There is room for more than one talented person on the team. There is no place for a competition over who is the best at anything. God doesn't use only the preacher who is the best; he uses many voices. The church isn't a place for only one person with any particular gift. As we earnestly seek the best gifts it makes no difference if the Lord uses you or someone else to fulfill his purposes.

At the more mundane level we are all different. If you feel negative emotions because someone has more attractive physical attributes than yourself you will experience a lot of pain. Someone will always be prettier, stronger, taller or better. Do the best you can with what you've got and you will be attractive enough. That may mean you need more exercise, nutrition, sleep or simply more time in front of the mirror.

Our consumer driven economy relies on envy. The new model smartphone is only incrementally better than the last model but on the day it hits the market thousands of people just have to have it. That creates money for the stockholders but it doesn't make much difference in the next phone call.

The world around us is always going to come up with something that looks better. Every year there are new clothing styles and colors season by season. And people crowd in front of the racks with longing eyes. It will never do for them to wait until the same piece of apparel goes on sale; they must have it now. Closets get bigger and bigger. Soon some people may need drive-in closets. But they won't be more content. In fact contentment will decrease with the increased number of choices.

It is time for believers to take a hard look at their lifestyles. Houses get bigger but contentment doesn't grow. People now have rooms in their houses they never enter or use while homelessness is all around. More food goes in the green waste bin than ever before while some people, even in the same communities, go silently hungry. No one person can feed everyone who gathers their food at the food bank but everyone can share a meal.

I believe that every believer should take at least one trip in their lifetime to a place where poverty rules. That could be another country or a part of your own country or city. It changes you when you observe it first hand. You create indelible memories. Children and teens need such a tour much more than they need a day at the newest theme park.

One of the best ways to crush creeping envy is to look to people who have much less and consider their plight. The emotion of compassion has a way of dissolving envy. A life of compassion will allow no room for material envy to grow.

Another way to diminish envy is to practice true generosity, not the counterfeit kind that gives something in hope of a return. True generosity gives for the sake of giving. Even when the gift isn't appreciated it brings a sense of wholeness; envy only brings a sense of emptiness. When you get used to being full why would you ever choose emptiness?

Jeremiah said, *"My people have committed two sins: They have forsaken me, the spring of living water,and have dug their own cisterns, broken cisterns that cannot hold water."* (Jeremiah 13:2)

Your Take

1. Honestly, how do you feel when someone else succeeds at something you wish for yourself? What is going on in your heart that you can't rejoice with someone who is rejoicing?

2. Do you truly appreciate the riches you have in Jesus? When do you invest time dwelling on that?
3. If the books were all open what would others see about how you set the example of joyful generosity in spirit and in material things?

Finish It!

Bundle it all together and make it your life's work. It is time for you to write your own story. You have nothing left to do between now and the grave but write a story. Make it a good one. Don't worry about the fact that others may not follow you. Cut a path that is worth following. That is your high calling so get to it!

~ 41 ~

Great Expectations

"... Christ loved the church and gave himself up for her to make her holy, cleansing her by the washing with water through the word, and to present her to himself as a radiant church, without stain or wrinkle or any other blemish, but holy and blameless."
(Ephesians 5:25-27)

In order for expectations to be great they must be realistic because otherwise they will be dashed expectations. So in terms of church life what can we realistically expect?

When a church puts all its hopes in its pastor, the expectations are not realistic. Conversely, when a pastor places all expectations on a majority of people in the church being totally involved, the expectations are not realistic either.

There must be a symbiotic relationship between the key influencers in the church and the pastor. Most pastors will give up on the church based on five vocal detractors who ought not to be the key influencers. Curiously, at the same time most pastors will accept a call to a new church they would never want to be a member of otherwise. These facts point in the opposite direction of a productive synergistic relationship.

While the length of pastoral tenure has increased over the past few decades, that has positive and negative implications. When the relationship is working it is a good thing; however, when it is stale and unproductive it will be hard to repair both now and in the future because old habits die hard.

For you as an individual, no matter what your role in the church you would do well to take Reinhold Neibuhr's prayer to heart. You probably know the first part but do you know the rest?

The Serenity Prayer

God grant me the serenity
To accept the things I cannot change;
Courage to change the things I can;
And wisdom to know the difference.
Living one day at a time;
Enjoying one moment at a time;
Accepting hardships as the pathway to peace;
Taking, as He did, this sinful world
As it is, not as I would have it;
Trusting that He will make all things right
If I surrender to His Will;
So that I may be reasonably happy in this life
And supremely happy with Him
Forever and ever in the next.
Amen.

Courage to change the things you can is the issue. You can have great expectations for yourself and fulfill them to a high degree. Make it your ambition to live out the "*one anothers*" personally. You can control that regardless of your role in the church. If you are a leader you can thereby set the example for others and be vocal about it to a few you take on to mentor. If you are the lowliest member you too can set the example and provide sideways coaching to other lowly members. Over time your living proof will probably bring you some graduation in influence and perhaps even graduation to leadership.

In the real world of your church the Pareto Principle applies. Eighty per cent of the church income comes from twenty percent of the people. Eighty percent of the volunteer hours comes from twenty percent of the people. If your church does better than that rejoice! Strive to do better than that by being in the twenty percent yourself and finding joy in the moments. Wishing for something that will never happen or at least hasn't happened yet is not something you can control. You need wisdom to see that.

At the same time, hold out the ideal of total involvement and sacrificial giving in keeping with income as the Scripture requires. (1 Corinthians 16:2) By your patient joyful example some will aspire to your level. A few will even supersede your productivity because they find the reasonable happiness Neibuhr prayed for.

You can place expectations on yourself. Organizationally and structurally your church may or may not improve. You can't really control that. Be a cheerleader for changes that put your church more in touch with the culture around you and for the programming and physical enhancements that will bring glory to God. But put your personal life change way in front of all that.

It is a conundrum as to how your church could ever become a "*radiant church without spot or wrinkle*" given who the members are! But in the great hope that is exactly what Jesus intends to do. Isn't that just a multiplier of the concept of you becoming a perfect person? You hope for personal perfection some glorious day so why not have great expectations for your local church as well?

The best answer about the methodology or means of that pursuit to perfect is in Ephesians 5:26, "*... cleansing her by the washing with water through the word...*" It isn't about a philosophy of ministry, organizational structure, use of contemporary forms and means or some other new concept. It is about the continual washing provided by the word. A Word saturated church has the probability of becoming more radiant.

Words matter. The people of the church are in possession of words in their own language and thus can expound on the Word of God. Reading is critical. There is evidence that reading moves the soul more than the passive engagement of watching or listening. That may be because when a person is reading the pace is dictated by the individual and there is more opportunity to slow the pace and ponder or increase the pace for coverage. You have to read to lead. If a person is not a reader, they must get over that and become one. Teach people to start slowly and read a paragraph a day if that is all they can muster at first.

You are to be commended because you have got this far in this book. Only about one in five get this far in any book and you have shown yourself to be in the top twenty percent. However, in reading this book it is probably the only one of its kind you have ever seen. Even though these "*one anoth-*

ers" are somewhat well known in the church, there is very little written about them.

We kept the chapters short. The reason for that is that you can use these chapters one at a time for personal introspection, spousal discussion, small group interaction or even sermon topics. You have the opportunity to pass the book along or better copy a four page chapter to share with a friend. Take a friend to coffee and read a chapter to them. Then ponder it together. You might even ask yourself the three questions at the end of each chapter. Imagine the difference if the twenty percenters in your church all did this with someone each week!

Now that you are here, what do you expect of yourself? Set some simple great expectations, meet the behavior objectives you have set for yourself and see how far it takes you!

~ 42 ~

Let's Get Practical

***"My grace is sufficient for you, for my power is made perfect in weakness."* (2 Corinthians 12:9)**

***"Finally, brothers and sisters, rejoice! Strive for full restoration, encourage one another, be of one mind, live in peace. And the God of love and peace will be with you."* (2 Corinthians 13:11)**

Probably by now you are overwhelmed by all that these "*one anothers*" imply. If not, perhaps you weren't really paying attention! It is a magnificent pursuit that requires your full attention every day. This must engage your thoughts, your feelings and your actions. We live in the day Jeremiah looked forward to, "*I will put my law in their minds and write it on their hearts. I will be their God, and they will be my people. No longer will they teach their neighbor, or say to one another, 'Know the Lord,' because they will all know me, from the least of them to the greatest," declares the Lord. 'For I will forgive their wickedness and will remember their sins no more.'*" (Jeremiah 31:33-34) This life changing and empowering Gospel is already written inside every true believer. Now it's time to change!

Many around you claim to be living a Christian life because they have what they perceive to be a clean moral life – or at least relatively so by what the public can see. But you now know it is more than avoiding nine or ten naughty sins. Christian living is proactive. You now know that it is much more than not harming others; it is helping others move away from harms. You now know first hand that the defensive question asked by Cain in the garden has an affirmative answer. The question, "*Am I my brother's keeper?*" (Genesis 4:9) must be met with a resounding "Yes!"

There are simple things you can do to keep yourself moving in the right direction. Here are some of them.

1. **Ingest the Word**. Make it a habit to ground yourself in the Bible. Bible reading has dropped like a stone in western civilization. You carry the Bible in your pocket or at least you can. There are several Bible apps. Most of them will even read the Bible to you. If you have a daily commute get your ear buds in and start listening if you find reading to be tedious. Try going over the same chapter each day for a month until your soul is saturated with it.
2. **Learn to Pray.** ACTS. Adoration. Confession. Thanksgiving. Supplication. Start your day right by talking to the Lord early. Link up your morning routine with prayer and the Word. You can pray while you brush your teeth. Two minutes. Thirty seconds on each of four sections of your teeth. Imagine that! Thirty seconds for reach part of ACTS!
3. **Find a Mentor.** There is someone in your church you admire who is about ten years down the road in front of you. Ask that person if you can have a conversation with them once a week and ask questions about how to live. Specifically ask that person the best ways they have found to live out the "*one anothers*." You can do this over the phone or face-to-face. Share your burdens and at the same time carry your mentor's burdens with you.
4. **Become a Mentor**. Find someone in your church who demonstrates a desire to be faithful, available and teachable. This person needs to be a phase of life behind you, not beside you. In your younger years a year or two seems like a long way behind. As life unfolds the age differential is usually from 10-20 years, You don't want to invest in a know-it-all. They will try to reverse mentor you. Wait until the hard knocks of life catch up with such a person before you try to help. If you don't that person will drive you nuts!
5. **Get a System.** If you don't systematize you will be left to randomize. And if you wait until the mood hits you to do something important it won't hit often enough. Think in terms of the God-given seven day cycle. Especially highlight the one day He told you to highlight. Sunday is your best day to start to systematize your spiritual life.
6. **Make Sunday Special.** Sunday is not for grass cutting, car washing, shopping and catching up. Sunday is for rest and worship. Reset your

heart and mind every Sunday. Follow Jesus and get up early on Sunday. The rest of your household can be lazy if they choose but not you. Hit your stride early. Get out the door earlier. Get to the meeting earlier. Get your game face on earlier. Your game face is the one with the smile and the energy. You can be sure Satan will throw logs across your path. Move them away and be the example.

7. **Review the One Anothers**. Once a week (at least) ask yourself how you are demonstrating self-donation and self-sacrifice to those around you. This goes beyond your family even if it starts there. Galatians 6:10 is clear. You have an obligation to do good to all people but especially to those in your church. Start by thinking about love every time and then cycle through all the others. Greeting and hospitality are the repeats so make them a special feature of your thinking as you plan ahead.
8. **Control Your Calendar.** Have you noticed how busy you and everyone else is this week? The secret is that nobody is busy six weeks from now. Take advantage of that and book yourself into other people's lives six weeks in advance. You can do this with your mentoring, both upline with your mentor and downline with your mentees. Stay way out in front. If you have to reschedule later it is easy. Canceling an appointment puts time back in your availability pattern.
9. **Stay Hungry.** You are the only one who can stir yourself toward your goal. Athletes live their lives striving to win championships and many never win but they keep striving. 1 Corinthians 9:24-27 tells you how hungry Paul was and he told us, "*Follow my example, as I follow the example of Christ to follow him as he follows Christ.*" (1 Corinthians 11:1)
10. **Live in Bright Colors**. Make your life interesting, fun and colorful by taking on new challenges at every phase along the way. Once you are past fifty your hormone supply starts to diminish. You will have to be bright more because of your will than the brain chemistry that drives you. Don't lament that fact. Prove what you are made of deep inside your heart. Paint for the joy of painting, not for the reward.
11. **Subjugate the Clubs**. There are clubs, teams and associations for keeners in every field of endeavor. Keep them under control. That includes the Christian clubs. They must take a back seat to your local church. Get your church calendar into your calendar first and let everything else work around that because the church is the only club, team or association ordained by God.
12. **Spread the Word.** You were called to fish for people. (Matthew 4:19)

That is the first "*follow me*" of Jesus. Learn how to structure your life so that your lifestyle and your words demonstrate you hare a commercial fisherman for the Lord. It isn't that hard. It only takes nine words.

Do you remember the story of Sam from the chapter "I'll Encourage You"? If not, check out Wendy's Take on him once again. We are constantly marveling at God's work in this man's life.

Gary has been suggesting many times that he watch The Gospel of John movie on YouTube. Well, last Sunday he finally sat down for three hours and took it all in. Soon after, he exclaimed to Gary that he saw it and wants to watch it over again. He remarked, "It made me tear up!" Is that good or what? He also has taken Gary's advice to read his Bible five minutes a day and spend five minutes a day cleaning his home. In the last couple of months at our church he has asked the blessing out loud for our lunch together. We were so pleased to hear him speak to Jesus as if he were in the restaurant with us. A mutual friend of ours is going through a marriage explosion. Sam asked for his phone number so he could give him a call to encourage him since he has walked in his shoes before. Our friend in the troubled marriage teared up when he got the call particularly when so many others have not taken the initiative to connect.

Now that is how a developing Christian life should be according to the New Testament "*one anothers*." We are watching Sam bubble up more and more as we bubble up ourselves. That is extremely exciting and gratifying!

Don't miss out on the great adventure! Bubble Up Church!

Extra Resources

Contact me at gary@garyvcarter.com and ask for a link to the extra resources to help you with your "*one another*" quest. I will get you the help you need – much of it for free. In many cases, there are people, books and courses I can point you to that will supply you all the help you need. And then it is up to you to live it out!

The 62 One Anothers

References in Book Order

Where there is more than one similar statement, the subsequent statement(s) are grouped together under a numbered title before continuing on with the New Testament book order. You may have seen a list of 59 one anothers originally gathered by Dr. Carl George. That list includes a few of the other one anothers that are not based on the word "*allélón*" and he omitted a few references. There are actually 100 uses of the word but only the ones that apply as instruction to us are included here. As you can see by this list, if we cancel out the duplicates we have a list of 36 to live by.

1. "*... be at peace with each other.*" .... Mark 9:50
2. Don't Grumble (2)
    - "*Stop grumbling among yourselves ...*" .... John 6:43
    - "*Don't grumble against one another ...*" .... James 5:9
3. "*... wash one another's feet.*" .... John 13:14
4. Love one another (16)
    - "*Love one another.*" .... John 13:34
    - "*... love one another.*" .... John 13:34
    - "*... love one another.*" .... John 13:35
    - "*Love each other ...*" .... John 15:12
    - "*Love each other.*" .... John 15:17
    - "*... love one another ...*" .... Romans 13:8
    - "*... love ... for each other ...*" .... 1 Thessalonians 3:12
    - "*... love each other.*" .... 1 Thessalonians 4:9
    - "*... love ... for one another ...*" .... 2 Thessalonians 1:3
    - "*... love one another deeply...*" .... 1 Peter 1:22
    - "*... love one another.*" .... 1 John 3:11
    - "*... love one another ...*" .... 1 John 3:23

- "*... love one another ...*" ....1 John 4:7
- "*... love one another.*" ....1 John 4:11
- "*... love one another ...*" ....1 John 4:12
- "*... love one another.*" ....2 John 1:5

5. Encourage One Another (4)
   - "*... encouraged by each other's faith.*" ....Romans 1:12
   - "*... encourage one another ...*" .... 1 Thessalonians 4:18
   - "*... encourage one another ...*" ....1 Thessalonians 5:11
   - "*... encourage one another daily ...*" ....Hebrews 3:13
6. Belong as One (2)
   - "*... each member belongs to all the others ...*" ....Romans 12:5
   - "*... same attitude of mind toward each other ...*" ....Romans 15:5
   - "*... for we are all members of one body.*" ....Ephesians 4:25
7. "*Be devoted to one another ...*" ....Romans 12:10
8. "*Honor one another ...*" ....Romans 12:10
9. "*Live in harmony with one another.*"..................................Romans 12:16
10. "*... stop passing judgment on one another.*"........................Romans 14:13
11. "Accept one another ..." ....Romans 15:7
12. "*... instruct one another.*" ....Romans 15:14
13. Greet one another (4)
    - "*Greet one another ...*"..Romans 16:16
    - "*Greet one another ...*".. 1 Corinthians 16:20
    - "*Greet one another ...*".. 2 Corinthians 13:12
    - "*Greet one another ...*"..1 Peter 5:14
14. "*Stop depriving one another ...*"................................... 1 Corinthians 7:5
15. "*... all eat together.*" ....1 Corinthians 11:33
16. "*... have equal concern for each other.*".................... 1 Corinthians 12:25
17. "*... serve one another ...*"..Galatians 5:13
18. "*... bite and devour each other ...*" ....Galatians 5:15
19. "*... destroyed by each other.*"..Galatians 5:15
20. "*... provoking and envying each other.*" ....Galatians 5:26
21. "*Carry each other's burdens ...*"..Galatians 6:2
22. Bear With One Another (2)
    - "*... bearing with one another in love.*" ....Ephesians 4:2
    - "*Bear with each other ...*"..Colossians 3:13
23. "*Be kind and compassionate to one another ...*" ....Ephesians 4:32
24. Forgive One Another (2)
    - "*... forgiving each other ...*" ....Ephesians 4:32
    - "*... forgive ... one another.*" ....Colossians 3:13
25. "*Submit to one another ...*" ....Ephesians 5:21

26. "*... value others above yourselves ...*"................................Philippians 2:3
27. "*Do not lie to each other ...*" ....Colossians 3:9
28. "*... build each other up ...*" ....1 Thessalonians 5:11
29. "*... do what is good for each other ...*" .... 1 Thessalonians 5:15
30. "*... spur one another on ...*" ....Hebrews 10:24
31. "*... do not slander one another.*"... James 4:11
32. "*... confess your sins to each other ...*" .... James 5:16
33. "*... pray for each other ...*" .... James 5:16
34. "*Offer hospitality to one another ...*"..1 Peter 4:9
35. "*... humility toward one another ...*"...1 Peter 5:5
36. "*... we have fellowship with one another ...*"..............................1 John 1:7

Scripture References

References in Alphabetical Order

Numbered Books

A

C

D

E

G

H

J

L

M

P

R

T

Other Books by Kainos Enterprises

Visit www.kainos.store for these and a growing list of other fine titles

In Alphabetical Order

Baptism - The Powerful Step - A Pastoral Quest: by Gary V Carter

Church Health - The Essential Personal and Organizational Facets: Gary V Carter

Church Ministry - How to Crank It Up without Getting Cranky: by Gary V Carter

Drop By Sometime - The simple and effective method to reach newcomers for your church: by Gary V Carter

From Sermon to eBook in a Jiffy: by Gary V Carter

From the Couch to the Stage: by Sara Burton (secular)

Hot Brass Tacks - Can a dozen statements change your world? by Gary V Carter

How to Reproduce Your Church - Helpful hints on church planting and pitfalls to be avoided: by Gary V Carter, Timothy Starr

How to Talk to Strangers in Church - Repairing the simple deficiency that may be strangling your church: by Gary V Carter

Kacie's Pass - A twenty year panorama of the journey of experiencing a stillborn child: by Sara and Chris Burton

Leadership Styles: The 6 styles you must master to lead a church: by Gary V Carter

Life on the Zipline - From Fear to Awe: by Gary Carter, Warwick Cooper, Robin Pifer, Douglas Rowley

Look at the Birds … Consider the Flowers: by Wendy Carter

Pain or No Pain - The Chiropractic Connection: by Wendy Carter on chiropractic benefits (secular)

Pastor Search 411 - Find the Right Pastor: by Lance Johnson

Positive Association - How to boost your church ministry through your extended team: Godfrey Thorogood, Gary V Carter

See You Next Week! The Ultimate Church Welcoming System: by Gary V Carter, Robin Pifer

The Complete Man: by Gary V Carter

The Pastor's Manifesto: by Gary V Carter

www.ingramcontent.com/pod-product-compliance
Lightning Source LLC
LaVergne TN
LVHW090939080826
845145LV00003B/819

* 9 7 8 0 9 6 8 5 4 2 7 5 0 *